Words of Praise for *Putting Everyday Life on the Page*

"A refreshing break from the rule-obsessed 'how to teach students to write' manuals that litter the educational marketplace. What better way to teach students to write than through their own experiences, their own senses, their own feelings of mystery, wonder, excitement, and dread! Let teachers everywhere use this book to make new Kafkas, Woolfs, and Ellisons, and to awaken in every student a love for making words that just sing off the page!"

Thomas Armstrong, Author of
The Multiple Intelligences of Reading and Writing

"This book is packed with lessons ready for use."

Jim D'Acosta, Teacher, Fairfield Warde High School, Fairfield, CT

"Lucky for all young writers, Marc Levitt is now making his storytelling talents available to educators in this practical and user-friendly book. Teachers across the curriculum will find Marc's suggestions innovative and helpful as he describes how to transition students through the writing process. Always student-centered, Marc invites us to keep children and their interests at the heart of writing. In a time when many schools are focused on teaching and testing technical skills in language arts, Marc reminds us that the purpose of writing is to have purpose, and that children need to learn to write so they can do on paper what they are so good at anyway—telling their stories. Thanks so much, Marc!"

Pat Cordeiro, Professor, Rhode Island College, Providence, RI

"Young writers often don't grasp what their teachers are asking them to do. The author offers many strategies to make abstract writing concepts more concrete."

Stacy Gardner Dibble, Fifth Grade Teacher/
Reading Coordinator, Prairie Elementary, Worthington, MN

"This book has some of the strongest writing prompts and examples I have read in a long time!"

Brenda Lynch, Spanish Teacher, Madison High School, SD

"This book is written from years of passionate experience in classrooms with students. It offers a multitude of great ideas for lessons."

Diane W. McDougal, Art Teacher, East High School, Cheyenne, WY

"Inventive and original, Marc Levitt's ideas actually put the fun back in writing—for teachers and for students."

Susan Ohanian, Senior Fellow, Vermont
Society for the Study of Education

"With Levitt's pre-writing and observing activities, targeted lessons, and simple strategies that create a desire to write, teaching students to write better is not only possible but fulfilling and fun."

R. James Stahl, Founder, *Merlyn's Pen* Magazine
and the New Library of Young Adult Writing

To my wife, Viera

Putting Everyday Life on the Page

Inspiring Students to Write, Grades 2–7

Marc Levitt

Corwin Press
A SAGE Company

Photos by Viera Levitt.

For information:

Corwin Press
A SAGE Company
2455 Teller Road
Thousand Oaks,
California 91320
www.corwinpress.com

SAGE Pvt. Ltd.
B 1/I 1 Mohan Cooperative
Industrial Area
Mathura Road, New Delhi 110 044
India

SAGE Ltd.
1 Oliver's Yard
55 City Road
London, EC1Y 1SP
United Kingdom

SAGE Asia-Pacific
Pte. Ltd.
33 Pekin Street #02–01
Far East Square
Singapore 048763

Printed in the United States of America.

Library of Congress Cataloging-in-Publication Data

Levitt, Marc.
Putting everday life on the page : inspiring students to write, grades 2–7/Marc Levitt.
p. cm.
Includes index.
ISBN 978-1-4129-6531-6 (cloth)
ISBN 978-1-4129-6532-3 (pbk.)
1. English language—Composition and exercises—Study and teaching (Elementary) 2. English language—Composition and exercises—Study and teaching (Middle school) 3. Creative writing (Elementary education) 4. Creative writing (Middle school) I. Title.

LB1576.L498 2009 372.62′3—dc22 2008021941

This book is printed on acid-free paper.

08 09 10 11 12 10 9 8 7 6 5 4 3 2 1

Acquisitions Editor: Carol Chambers Collins
Editorial Assistant: Brett Ory
Production Editor: Veronica Stapleton
Copy Editor: Jovey Stewart
Typesetter: C&M Digitals (P) Ltd.
Proofreader: Dennis W. Webb
Indexer: Kathleen Paparchontis
Cover Designer: Lisa Riley

Contents

Preface

I was a reluctant student at best. While compliant, certainly in my younger years, my interest in schoolwork was never imbued with the passion I had for baseball. By the time I was seven, I knew each of the stadiums where the then 16 teams played. Not too much later, I knew batting averages and home run totals, birthdates, and occasional hometowns of my favorite ballplayers. I studied the back of the baseball cards bought each week at Barenberg's candy store up on the Boulevard. I read the Yankee yearbook cover to cover. I argued the merits of one player versus the other and one team against another, not with the statistical acumen of today's Bill James' obsessed scholars but good enough for a grade school kid in those statistically "primitive" days.

When I did have to work for school, I'd skid through my math problems, reading assignments, penmanship, or grammar like a fried egg on Teflon. To allow those students who were more serious than I to finish their assignments without interruption, my teachers let me indulge in my other passion (other than the lovely, Susan Silverman!), maps! I was permitted to look at, trace, and copy maps. I loved the shapes of continents and countries. I loved their irregularities; the squiggles that I now know as inlets and isthmuses. I loved the bays, the lakes, and how some states like Colorado, Kansas, and the Dakotas seemed completely geometric while others, like Michigan or Florida had funny pieces of land that seemed to "stretch out" into the territory of other states. I loved looking at how South America must have at one time nestled into the Western coast of Africa. (I figured that out myself!) And Greenland always looked *sooo* big! And why was it "green" if it was so far north? (Given the current warnings of global warming, maybe there was something prescient in its naming, come to think of it.)

When I graduated from college in 1971, I moved first to Seattle and then to San Francisco. Needing a job, I answered an ad in the paper for a nursery school teacher. Having had a couple of education classes at the urging of my father, I applied for and got the job. It was part-time. I was essentially the male role model at a single parent (mostly women), feminist, socialist cooperative nursery school in a pink building in Noe Valley, a small neighborhood in the city. The school was on the first floor of what had been a private house. The upstairs was rented to one of the parents and her child, two wonderful people who would come sweeping (and sleepily) down from their quarters in lovely pink silk bathrobes and/or colorfully and creatively mixed and matched outfits that might include rainbow colored socks, long gowns, and blue jeans. Not knowing much about teaching, I did two things. I watched to make sure that everyone felt included, and I created as many experiences for the children as I could, both in school and out. Without much in the way of theory or experience, I instinctively felt that by taking time to observe I would get to know the children; their likes and dislikes as well as their social and intellectual needs. Additionally, I felt that our various forays into the world would stimulate their senses, curiosity, and joy for coming to and being in school.

I tell these anecdotes so that you can begin to get a sense of who you're going to be spending some time with . . . a middle-aged, married man who carries around vivid memories of what he learned, how he learned, and therefore what was and still is important to him about teaching and learning. I forgot who said this, but I like it . . . "School is a six-hour interruption from learning." While this is certainly an exaggeration, it has some truth to it or at least it did for me. My interests as a child lay outside what was being taught about in school. I was interested in sports, in social relations, and as I got older, in contemporary politics and culture. While school occasionally utilized and intersected with what I knew and what I was interested in, most of the times what I "had" to learn and what I was interested in seemed at best unrelated and at worse, at variance with what was being taught in school.

This is not to say that school wasn't valuable to me or that I didn't learn to write, read, do math, learn about isosceles triangles and paramecium, as well as about Albania and Turkey, the two countries I chose to do an oral report on in fifth grade. (I still remember my mother worried about being photographed going into the then Maoist Albanian Embassy as she helped gather resources for me.) No, I learned and I am thankful for the education I had. But it could have been a lot easier, and it could have been a lot more fun if only I had been really "noticed," talked to and not at, and if I had been respected and acknowledged for the knowledge and interests I brought to school every day.

I was smart, as are most children. Author Howard Gardner's work affirmed what I already sensed from my experiences as a young person. Roy got 70s on his report card but had the funniest sense of humor with great timing. Lee couldn't sit still in class and yet was always able to organize kids for a game. Penny wouldn't do her math but could she ever draw . . . etc., etc., etc. We all have stories like this, don't we?

So, continuing my history, after my first teaching experience and another of shorter duration, I realized that I probably was not "hard-wired" for the teaching profession and became interested in and went on to become a performer, writer, and an arts educator. I created and toured with an "old time" medicine show, juggling, playing music, doing magic and comedy in schools, theaters, and fairs throughout the United States. I became a storyteller, performed a number of one-person shows, and then created and directed a museum school in an inner city Providence, Rhode Island, school. Here, students and artists created museum-quality exhibits based on inquiries about their former factory building and their multicultural and multi-use neighborhood. While doing this work, I developed and refined many of my theories concerning "real-world" presentations, inquiry, and the importance of taking advantage of what's around you. I've also hosted, written, and directed two long-running radio shows and have made a documentary film on the Narragansett Native American stonewall building tradition. Additionally, I've had the good fortune to work with great musicians on the historical narratives I've written about tenement houses, watersheds, rivers, and farms. Currently, I'm traveling around the world, performing and teaching workshops in, among other things, writing, diversity education, and human rights.

While my educational philosophy has evolved—and I guess both my ideas and practices have become more refined with age—the foundation for my knowledge and for the work that I do are the lessons I learned as a mostly lethargic student; ones that I used as far back as my first teaching experience: to observe, utilize, and build upon what I notice in those I'm teaching. I bring this understanding to you by way of this book with the humility of someone who knows how hard you work and how much you care.

Acknowledgments

We all learn and create within an environmental context that includes people as well as the built and un-built world. We are affected by all of it. Recognizing the immensity of thanking everyone and everything, I do however want to give special thanks to a few: To Corwin Press and its publisher, Robb Clouse; to my editor, Carol Collins; and to Brett Ory, her editorial assistant; production editor, Veronica Stapleton; and copy editor, Jovey Stewart, all of whom recognized something in my work they thought others would care about; to my wife, Viera, for the book's photos; to all of the people who read and critiqued earlier versions of this work; to those who put their compliments on the cover and inside this book; to Mr. Kiernan, the advisor to my high school newspaper who was a teacher I could aspire to become; to the many wonderful teachers and principals I've worked with over the years; and of course to the children I've been associated with, who continue to prove me correct when I trust them to understand deeply, care intensely, and to be able to laugh along the way.

PUBLISHER'S ACKNOWLEDGMENTS

Corwin Press acknowledges with gratitude the important contributions of the following manuscript reviewers:

Emme Barnes
Literacy Facilitator
Hawk Ridge/Charlotte
Mecklenburg Schools
Charlotte, NC

Jim D'Acosta
High School Social Studies
Teacher, NBCT
Fairfield Warde High School
Fairfield, CT

Stacy Gardner Dibble
Fifth Grade Teacher/
Reading Coordinator
Prairie Elementary
Worthington, MN

Rosemary Fryer
English Teacher/Project Director
Heritage High School
Vancouver, WA

Brenda Lynch
Spanish Teacher
Madison Central School District
Madison, SD

Stephanie Malin
Elementary Instructional Coach
Nancy Ryles Elementary
Beaverton, OR

Diana W. McDougal
Art Educator
East High School
Cheyenne, WY

About the Author

Marc Levitt is a writer/storyteller/consultant who tours throughout the United States and to more than 35 countries. He has created one person historical shows, musically enhanced historical and ecological narratives, and award-winning audio stories in addition to producing plays and a documentary film on Narragansett (Native American) stonemasons. Marc Levitt lives with his wife, Viera, a contemporary art curator and photographer, in Wakefield, Rhode Island. Mr. Levitt can be reached at *MarcLevitt.org*

Introduction

Too often, teaching writing has been reduced to a series of educator-generated rules or prescriptions designed to "unpack" what it means to be a good writer and then simply to share those rules with students. The goal, increasingly, has been to produce successful test takers. For example, at a school where I often work, students were studying genres and at a particular moment were working on fantasy. Outside our school's windows there's an armory built at the turn of the 20th century. It looks like a fort, literally like some sort of 13th century English fort (at least how I imagine an old English fort to look). When I asked teachers whether or not their students were given the opportunity to look out the window and to use the building as an inspiration for their stories, none had. Their reason was simple and clear. "We just don't have time to do it. We have to get students ready for the test."

These are good, in fact some are very good teachers, all of whom have the students' best interests at heart. But teachers, principals, and superintendents are under such pressure to "teach to the test," they sometimes have difficulty seeing the forest for the trees. They are asked to march through genres like Sherman marching through the South. Each genre is a city that needs to be burned on the way to the great ocean of accountability. The students, I'm sure, often feel like they are on one of those European tours where you spend just enough time in a city to take a few photos before moving on to the next destination. Teachers are too often asked to teach writing through textbook-generated rubrics pasted onto our student's minds and hung throughout the classroom like flags. This approach, in my opinion, is destined to fail. I don't mean to imply that some students won't learn to write in this way. What I mean is this . . .

When we teach writing by pasting a set of do's and don'ts onto our students' compliant and at times non-compliant minds, it's like creating a façade for a house held up by termite-attacked timbers. The "house" might look good for the real estate listings (tests), but ultimately we are not really paying attention to the basic deficiencies in the "structure" itself; in the case of writing instruction, to the deficiencies in our students' thinking skills.

If we continue to teach writing by prioritizing façade over the soundness of our students' intellectual foundations, we fail to use the opportunity given to us to teach deep, creative, critical, confident, and empowered thinking.

I am not saying that using rubrics is necessarily "bad." It's just incomplete. Rubrics do provide students with the opportunity to understand what is expected of them and help to make grading more transparent. The problem with rubric-centered teaching, however, is that it is often set unrealistically and harmfully "high," the origins of the rubrics are hidden, and it is too often disconnected from the language and experience of the students we are teaching. Students rarely have a hand in helping to determine which rules to follow. Rubrics are often just "there" and students are expected to follow them as if they were the "Ten Commandments of Writing" and are supposed to measure their own writing by these seemingly immutable, universal, and "G—d-given" standards. Because of this, students understand these rules superficially but don't often internalize them. They are flat, static, alien and as I've said, don't encourage deep and critical thinking. If students don't feel they have participated in the creation of rules, unless their peers and their teachers have had a hand in generating these rules, they are less likely to internalize and *really* understand them. Therefore, there is less likelihood that these lessons will ever be transferable, "played with," or individualized. A rule is a rule, is a rule, and kids can certainly "spit" them back at you. But is this what we want? Do we want students to write as if they were "painting by numbers"? Do we want writing to follow a formula but be devoid of energy, creativity, and individuality?

I would hope the answer is, "No, of course not." We want our students to be able to write, think, and problem solve creatively. We want their writing to express their unique voices and at the same time to follow certain conventions that will make their writing attractive and comprehensible for their intended audience. We want our teaching to empower our students to live a life that is satisfying, challenging, and fulfilling.

Perhaps before we go on, we need to "check in" and ask ourselves a question to make sure we are "on the same page." What *are* we teaching writing for anyway? I know that seems like a question whose answer is self-evident. You might answer, "We are teaching students to write so they can have the tools that will help them be successful." OK, now the next question . . . What do you mean when you say "successful"? "To be able to function well in the society," you might say. OK, what does it take to be successful? "Well, writing and reading," you might answer. But, if you really thought about it for a second and thought about the times when you felt that you have successfully managed your life, you might also conclude that you needed other skills as well . . . creativity, confidence, patience, diligence, and social skills to help you to achieve what you consider success.

So, following this logic, we are destined to *fail* as writing instructors if we continue to teach writing by reducing it to a list of teacher or textbook-generated commands. By teaching in this way, we practically insure that many of our students will attain neither the confidence nor the intellectual and social flexibility needed to become successful adults. Additionally, we make *our* jobs harder and harder as we continually attempt to graft these writing "truths" onto our students' brains without their input, mutual exploration, and discovery. Engaged students are better-behaved students. They might be noisy and chaotic at times, but it is not be because they are bored and attempting to subvert instruction, instead it is because genuine intellectual engagement is often passionate and messy.

HOW DO WE ACCOMPLISH THIS?

Students need to understand that writing well is not simply a result of following mysteriously generated rules, but that rules and convention derive from an understanding of language and composition *they* can actually grasp internally. The more students embrace an *inner* understanding of linguistic conventions, the more they will take ownership in these conventions and the more easily they will be able to adopt them to fit various circumstances.

My basic idea is this . . .

> When teaching writing, it is important to identify, acknowledge, build upon, and utilize the experiences and knowledge of your students.

For instance, when teaching how to begin a story, ask students what they already know about how a movie trailer works. When we teach sequential thinking, ask students to identify some of the activities they do sequentially, like a relay race or brushing their teeth. When teaching topic selection, tap into the everyday experiences of childhood as sources for their stories like, for instance, when they got lost. Students will understand and really internalize the craft of writing if you are able to demonstrate the parallels between what you are trying to teach and what your students have experienced in everyday life.

This book is about how to teach writing by acknowledging and taking advantage of what students already know. This book is about empowering students to realize that *they* can be "co-creators" of their own understanding of what *good* writing is. This book is about realizing that we are not teaching "just" writing but that we are teaching thinking skills, skills that will prepare students not just to be successful on tests, but for life. This book is about "composting the intellectual soil" in preparation for planting the seeds of the writer's craft. This book is about helping students to feel that their writing is important and meaningful and not simply a chore imposed from the "outside."

> Remember, we learn not only by what we are taught, but also by *how* we are taught. The delivery system for learning is every bit as important as *what* we are learning.

Putting Everyday Life on the Page will have chapters devoted to different aspects of the writer's craft: Beginnings, Sequential Thinking, Observation and Description, Characters, Place, and Endings. It will also have a chapter dedicated to how to establish a culture in your classroom that encourages writing and another on how to motivate students by finding ways to make student writing meaningful and purposeful.

While this book is valuable for all those who are teaching writing, the targeted audience is Grades 2–7. I have not delineated specific grades for the various suggested activities. You know your student's abilities better than I do and targeting certain exercises for certain grades falls into the category of "prescriptive learning" that I'm trying to avoid. Additionally, I've made a point of not specifically mentioning ELL (English Language Learners). This book is about taking advantage of and building on the experiences that students bring into the classroom. It goes without saying that this includes the rich and diverse experiences of those students who have moved to the United States from other countries. I vividly remember the excitement and interest generated at the Museum School, when we created a "Hall of Immigration" and invited students to bring in, create exhibitions of, and labels for cans of food eaten and cooking utensils used in their households, as well the rich writing that came from discussions of their first impressions of the United States.

Putting Everyday Life on the Page will, I hope, give you some new ways to excite your students about writing and help to make your job easier and more enjoyable. Please use the ideas in this book not as prescriptions to be meticulously followed but as intellectual trampolines that will help you experiment and improvise. I am also very interested to learn about your experiences utilizing this book. I am setting aside part of my Web site (*MarcLevitt.org*) that will allow all of us to share with each other, ideas, and activities generated from this book.

Remember, writing is above all a technology. Because we take it for granted, because it has always been around us, we forget how weird and abstract it really is. We are making letters that correspond to sounds, that when put together form words and sentences which, as best as we can, reproduce experiences, thoughts, feelings, etc., that we want to convey. Putting these sounds together on paper to make sense of and to describe an experience is difficult work. It is being made more difficult, in my opinion, by the pressures surrounding its teaching and accountability. Throwing water into a field might let you get wet if you jump into the puddle you've just created, but it doesn't mean you will have a place to swim. A pool needs to be built and water added. We can get students to follow the rules, but without "building the pool," we make our job and our student's work more difficult, less fulfilling, and ultimately not as sustainable.

I hope that you enjoy this book and thanks for giving it a chance. One bit of advice about reading it, if you don't mind from the great Lewis Carroll, "Where shall I begin, please, your Majesty?" he asked. "Begin at the beginning," the King said, gravely, "and go on till you come to the end: then stop."

Marc Levitt
Wakefield, Rhode Island

1

Beginnings

Getting the Audience to Pay Attention

Some begin a relationship with a handshake, some with a bow, some with a kiss on each cheek; others with the passing of a card, a request for a dance, a glance into the eyes. Beginnings happen in all kinds of ways and since we are beginning our relationship, I'd like to simply say, "Hello! Thanks for joining me."

The first thing we will discuss is (trumpet flourish, please . . . i.e., another way to *start*): How to *begin*!

The beginning of a story starts with a door opening into a room, a cartoon finger beckoning you into a bakery, a carnival barker inviting you to see the three-headed frog, etc. I always ask students to first understand that *everybody* is busy. Everybody! When you invite someone into your story, this truism must be considered in order to understand how difficult it is to take people away from their busy schedules and concerns into your writing. Being aware of this helps us create strategies to successfully invite a reader to "come inside the circus tent," that is, our writing. So, let's look first at what students already know about ways people bring others from everyday life into new situations and activities. How about a trailer for a movie, for instance?

What does the movie trailer do? It whets your interest for paying $10 (or more!) to go see a film. How? It shows you the most exciting parts of the film in a condensed form. It distills a film into its most intense moments. There are car chases, falling buildings, kisses exchanged, and fiery interactions fueled by anger, love, and lust. It makes you curious. What will happen to the character that tumbles through the sky? Will the beautiful woman choose the blond or black-haired young man? Will the detective find out where the bomb is in time to save the world from total destruction? Pay your $10 and see. Tune in next week and see part two. It makes you curious, doesn't it?

How do you teach kids to write an opening sentence that is as exciting as a movie trailer? How do you write an opening sentence that isn't a cliché like: "You'll never believe it when I tell you about . . ." Or overly wordy like: "I just had the most, wonderful, extraordinary, fantastic, amazing, surprising day of my life." Or completely ordinary like: "Can I tell you about my cat?" Or by *telling* and not *showing* like: "I was scared sitting on top of the Ferris wheel."

Writing opening sentences should be easy for kids. They already know about drama. Just listen to the games they play by themselves with stuffed animals, toy soldiers, and the like. When I was a child, I played with little plastic soldiers and lined them up against each other. Something always began the action: a shot, a fort crashing, or an act of *aggression* from one side on the other.

> What do *you* know that stimulates action or gets you interested in participating in an activity or an event? Spend a moment to think about this, because I'd like you to do it with your students.

How does an advertisement for a car work? Let's take a look. A family drives to some exotic location with the promise of new adventure. Didn't some car company actually use the great and inventive hook, "Tell better stories"? How about an ad or a brochure for a hotel in the Caribbean? I like the ads that simply compare the temperatures in say, St. Thomas, with the temperature in some cold northeastern city. Or perhaps, think about the look of contentment on the faces of tourists lounging in their bathing suits on the beach, a slight breeze ruffling their hair as they watch the waves curl gently onto the shore. What do these images promise? How do they attract you? In the constant bombardment of everyday sights and sounds (not to mention your own thoughts), a particular doorway is made enticing enough to lure you in. It seduces you to temporarily leave your everyday life and to enter a "story" someone else wants to share.

What are some famous openings? Charles Dickens in *A Tale of Two Cities*, "It was the best of times, it was the worst of times"; Franz Kafka in *The Metamorphosis*, "Gregor Samsa woke up and realized he had been turned into an insect"; James Baldwin in *Giovanni's Room*, "I stand at the window of this great house in the south of France as night falls, the night which is leading me to the most terrible morning of my life"; or in Genesis 1, "In the beginning G—d created the heavens and the earth."

What makes these so effective? What makes you want to continue reading? Curiosity, I suspect, first and foremost. A beginning sentence sets up some sort of drama that whets your curiosity.

What do students already know about that whets their appetite for adventure? It's important to find experiences students are familiar with; experiences they can dissect and analyze.

Let's think about the various *beginnings* students might be familiar with.

- The carnival barker trying to entice you to take a chance at knocking down some cloth clowns: "Step right up, Step right up. Wouldn't you like to come home with one of these dolls?"
- A newscaster previewing a news story coming up after the break. "After a break we are going to tell you about the man who discovered that his couch was dangerous to his health."
- The ice cream truck's jingle.
- The beginning of a horror movie . . . wind sneaking in through a crack in the window, footsteps, creaking gates, etc.
- The allure of a ringing cell phone or AOL's "You've got mail."
- The opening shot of a fireworks display.
- The smell of turkey roasting on Thanksgiving Day.
- The first few notes of a favorite song . . . I tend to think "My Girl" by the Temptations.
- The theme song of your favorite TV show.
- A big wrapped box with a bow on top.

- Hearing the parade's drums before you actually see anything.
- The beginning sounds and sights of a video game.

I'm sure that you and your students can add to this list. Now, let's look at what these *openings* have in common. What qualities do they share and what do they do differently?

Vivid sights, sounds, and smells . . . stimulate the senses, as well as the mind. The senses are in play. The mind is curious. You are woken up. An alarm clock! You're interested. The world is momentarily different. It becomes more vivid. The promise of something new is not only over the horizon; it's in front of your nose.

I always remember our delight as students when, in the middle of class and outside the window, we saw first the ropes of a scaffold beginning to move, followed by the shoes and legs of the man who was about to clean our windows. All "learning" stopped and our eyes became transfixed. It was out of the ordinary; unpredictable; a surprise!

HELPING STUDENTS CREATE COMPELLING OPENINGS

Start with a discussion about what your students already know about *openings* or beginnings. Remember, this does not necessarily mean the openings of stories, but rather techniques and tactics that, for instance, salesmen, advertising executives, and movie producers use to entice us to enter into a new environment. Have students make a list of these strategies and then look at them, talk about them and give a homework assignment to spend a few days looking for more. Direct students to pay attention to how these techniques work. Tell your students stories about how you became enticed or intrigued. If this sounds like too much time to devote, then take a little less time, but remember . . .

> This *is* teaching for the long term. This is not teaching just for the test, but it certainly will work for preparing kids for any kind of writing they ultimately do. Relax. Remember, you are not teaching formulas, but for understanding.

Once you've made a list of the above, now it's time to "unpack" what these techniques have in common. What senses were stimulated? How was curiosity stirred? What fears were 'surfaced'? What needs were pinpointed and utilized?

Consider these examples . . .

- The jingle of the ice cream man coming around: What senses are stimulated? Sound, taste, memory. Even if you are in the middle of

the most engaging game of say, basketball, once you hear that jingle, other needs are stimulated.
- A fireworks display: Boom! Sound and then, light and color. You got my attention!
- A barking dog, as you pass its fence: Sound, sight, and fear based on surprise and unpredictability.

Once you've put your list together, find ways to use these elements in different ways to attract attention, without writing a story.

Consider these examples . . .

- Have students come to the front of the room and get the class's attention *without* the use of words. Make a clear distinction between walking up to the front of the classroom and the moment when they are actually trying to hold the class's attention. Use sounds, looks, body movement, and so on, but no words. See how long each student can hold the attention of the class.
- Have students pretend they are on an infomercial, selling a product that they've invented. Have students draw attention to the product and to themselves as though they are being filmed.
- Have students create an opening for a horror movie. Write the first scene. You might want to suggest some locations . . . a house at night during a storm, an amusement park. If you have the facilities, have them actually create a video or a radio play, just of a beginning of a "tale of horror."
- Have students create a first sentence using different senses, one at a time . . . first smell, then sound, then taste, etc.
- Have students write two first sentences, one purposely boring and the other exciting. Have the class decide why they like one better than the other. I usually start by writing a few. The danger here is that kids will copy your sentence almost exactly. Just be aware of that as a possibility, as I'm sure most of you are.
- Have students look for opening sentences in literature that they like. You do the same. Then have a discussion with them about what they like about the openings.

Now, have your students write their own rubrics for the writing of first sentences, collectively or individually. For instance, children might generate the following criteria for an opening sentence:

- Stimulates one or more of the five senses
- Makes you curious about what's going to happen next
- Makes you feel something in your body and/or your mind
- Surprises you
- Demonstrates that we are *showing* and not just *telling*
- Connects to what follows

Take this mutually agreed upon rubric for opening sentences (of course that could include some you've suggested and that your students hadn't noticed) and put it in an easily visible place in your room. When students are writing and/or critiquing each other's writing, they can refer to the rubric they've generated.

Student understanding of *beginnings* is, well . . . just beginning. It's important to continuously refer back to the rubric that you've collectively created and every once in a while ask students if they've noticed anything new about "how to begin." You can do the same when you are creating and using rubrics for other elements of the writer's craft that we'll be discussing. Remember not to consider anything "the last word" and to help students feel that the rubric is always in the process of being created. This will help to encourage continual reflection about writing and a sense that its rules are mutually generated.

UNDERSTANDING THE *SHOWING* VERSUS *TELLING* DIFFERENCE

As students begin to understand that they have to "grab" an audience with their openings, they often try to do so with words that "mean" suspense. For instance, say they are starting a story about being on top of a Ferris wheel as the ride begins to shake, they might say, "I was nervous sitting on top of the Ferris wheel as the ride began to shake." Good start, but let's not end there. We'll look at how to build metaphors and similes later but for now, try to show the difference between reading the above opening and one that starts, "My stomach swirled like a merry-go-round out of control as the Ferris wheel shook beneath me." In one, the author is *telling* while in the other, the author is *showing*. In one, the writer is *holding back* while in the other, the writer is being *generous* with themselves.

Ask students to notice how each or similar pairs of endings make them feel. What *moves* them physically and viscerally, and what simply works in their *heads*. This body/mind criterion is a good one to introduce early as your students learn to write. Ask them to consider how their bodies felt when they hear one beginning or another. Do they like being affected in this way? Would they want to "read on" if they were affected in this way? Children know. We just have to help them notice and build upon this knowledge. *Showing* rather than *telling* is engaging with an experience versus detached observation. It is the difference between using a description that is specific to a situation and one where "one size fits all." It's a "made-to-order suit" versus one "off the rack."

So, now that we've "met"; now that we've had our *beginning*, maybe it's time to figure out what's next or to ask that well-known question; "Where are we going from here?" or "Let's not get ahead of ourselves," some of you might have replied at one or more times in your lives. Let's just see what happens next. Let's respect the natural sequence of events.

Speaking of which . . .

2

Sequential Thinking

Teaching Students to Think Logically and Make Story Sense

How often do we read a child's writing and wonder why some facts, sentences, or indeed entire paragraphs were either included or excluded? How often do we wonder where the main theme suddenly went? How often do we read an assignment when suddenly we are taken off the main road and, metaphorically speaking, sent down a dirt path out into the desert, losing confidence that we are ever going to make it back to the main "highway"?

We've all faced this. We all have wondered why some students who can actually tell a pretty logical story verbally cannot seem to get it down on paper. Haven't we all wondered why something that looks so clearly *illogical* is handed in as a finished product? In our Western culture, our comfort with *beginning, middle,* and *end,* with the sense that one thing, if not directly *causing* another is in some way related to another, seems almost to be *hardwired* into our brain. In this chapter, we will look at ways to help students *pay attention* to what they already know about this narrative structure and to build on it, so they can recreate it in their writing and notice when it is not there in the writing of others.

Let's first understand, of course, that what we get from our students is usually rushed off in order to get the teacher "off their backs." I will address this issue later in the section on purposeful writing. For now, let's assume that even writing with a student-generated purpose and an intended audience way beyond the eyes of the teacher will still have gaps in the narrative.

What is this sense of a sequence, of narrative order; this feeling of beginning, middle, and end that we, as adults, seem to understand almost instinctively but that most kids have a hard time comprehending? How can we teach it? How do we help our students realize that one sentence either does or doesn't follow from another and that one paragraph either supports or doesn't support a main idea of the story?

The first step toward helping students understand sequence is to look at where they find it in their everyday lives.

For instance, let's look at simple everyday tasks like brushing teeth, putting on and tying shoes, washing and drying dishes, baking cookies, downloading music into an MP3 player, walking to school, getting ready for school. By discussing these sequentially based activities, we make our students aware of what it *feels* like to live inside of and to participate in a sequence where each step has an essential role in getting to the next.

Have students make a list of all the activities they participate in or are familiar with where there is clearly a beginning, middle, and end. Have them describe, first verbally, then later through writing, the steps one takes when doing some of these activities. This can be lots of fun when student after student try to describe the various stages of, say, brushing one's teeth and inevitably leaves out some stage of the process, like turning on the faucet. While just one student is doing this activity, the others are working as well. They are thinking, remembering, and watching for mistakes in their peer's description. This kind of attention to the details of a sequence is invaluable since it makes intellectually "visible" what they already know internally about sequencing.

While someone is describing the sequence, it is also fun to have someone, or yourself, act out the different stages being articulated. This not only makes for some funny movement, but it points out how absurd a faulty sequential order can be. For instance, again with brushing teeth, the sight of an imaginary toothbrush left in the mouth, because a child has forgotten to say, "Take the toothbrush from the mouth," can produce quite a few giggles.

> Remember, students learn best when they have a positive emotional connection to what is being taught and with the way it is being taught!

Having students teach something is another way for them to grasp the inner logic of sequence. Allow them to prepare this activity the night before and certainly brainstorm about what knowledge and skills they might share. They can teach a board game, a card game, a recipe, a sport, text messaging, a video game, somersault, planting a seed, how to create a MySpace page or a Facebook site or upload a file to YouTube, etc. It goes without saying (but I will anyway) that students should avoid teaching their peers to do something inappropriate to the available space (for instance, making s'mores in the classroom). As you are preparing students for this activity, point out how important it is to include *all* of the steps of what they are trying to teach. Remind them that without one of the steps, their entire description might not make sense, for example, chocolate cookies without the chips, balloon animals without air in the balloons, text messaging without pushing the "send" button, planting a garden without watering the seeds. Actually, this could be a fun activity to do: discuss, draw, or take photos of "completed" activities but with one important step missing.

Another way to reinforce sequential thinking is to think about biographies. If a biography went from describing where someone was born, to their elementary, high school, and college experience, to them sitting on a rocking chair with gray hair on their porch surrounded by 10 youngsters, something would be missing. There certainly can be narrative reasons to go from childhood to being a grandfather in a story, but for the purpose of this chapter, I'm not looking at these more challenging and experimental ideas of narrative, time, and sequence.

Writing biographies, autobiographies, and creating timelines both personal and historical are great ways to continue your students' immersion in sequential thinking. For instance, have students bring in pictures from various stages of their lives (with description) and put them up somewhere in the classroom in chronological order. Or, do a timeline of your school's neighborhood or modes of transportation.

Sometimes to reinforce sequential thinking in an entertaining way, I play a game on the blackboard or whiteboard with students. I liken a sequence to building steps on a suspension bridge, perched over a river with, for dramatic effect, a shark under the water. Each step is a sentence to a story. If I miss a sentence, if I go from say, sentence two to four, without three, I will fall into the water and be eaten by the inaccurately situated animal. For instance, drawing the river on the board and of course the shark inside, I start . . .

Sentence 1: One day, I took a walk in the woods with my father.

Sentence 2: It was a cold day, and luckily we were both wearing warm clothes.

Sentence 3: I realized that it was starting to snow.
(I keep checking with the students as I create each step over the "river.")

Sentence 4: Suddenly a wolf jumped out from behind a large boulder.

Sentence 5: Luckily my dog chased it away.

If I'm lucky a student will yell out, "Where did the dog come from?" If not, I have to pause for second or two. I fall into the "river," get eaten by the shark, and I start another round, with the shark fatter this time around. This game can go on and on, and eventually you can have the students play . . . as a class . . . or as teams. They have to make up a six-sentence story, for example (this is an arbitrary though workable number), with a beginning and ending. You can start with the entire class first, picking a child to start the first sentence, then the second sentence, and so on. The only thing to watch out for here is not embarrassing a child whose contribution did not logically spring from the last sentence and who becomes the reason another "person" is fed to the shark. Students always enjoy this game and while they are doing it, they are obviously internalizing the logic of sequence.

Just a quick aside . . . as all of us as educators know, there is not one subject that should really be taught as a stand-alone. We can reinforce one discipline with knowledge from other disciplines. When I was in school, every once in a while something that was being taught in English (Dickens) was reinforced by something that was being taught in history (the Industrial Revolution). I still remember the "aha" moments when this would happen.

In teaching sequential thinking, we can easily recognize the benefits of teaching critical thinking. For instance, explain why or why not the following statement does or doesn't make sense for the benefit of debate; listen to and find the fault in someone's argument; or the old SAT-style question . . . "If x is to y as y is to z, then. . . ." These are all part of a mental regimen that will help students pay attention to and come to an inner understanding of the nature of sequence and the essence of logical thinking. When we teach our students to look for faults in logic or to find the fallacies in an argument, we are teaching them the critical thinking skills they need to use when they examine their own work for "gaps" in the sequential logic of their own writing.

TALKING ABOUT LITERATURE

It is important that students read a lot and that teacher generated questions follow the reading. Depending on the type of discussion and questions asked, this activity will also help reinforce critical and sequential thinking skills. For instance:

- What is the author's intent in writing the story?
- What are the main points the author is trying to convey?
- How do the characters and places in the story help to reinforce the main point of the story?
- Are there elements in the story you think are not necessary or take you away from the main story line?
- Are any parts of the story similar to things you have thought about or have experienced?
- Look at the big ideas in these stories to see how you would have told such a story based on events in your own life.

These kinds of questions are often a suggested part of many reading curriculums. I like it when these questions are posed as part of a group activity, sitting around in a "reader's circle." As we will talk about later, creating a culture of writing in your classroom not only creates opportunities to learn from one's peers but also makes it safe and attractive to be a "thinker." As part of this reader's circle, it is important to encourage students to share their own stories about themes introduced by the author being discussed. As the student narrates, everyone else in the circle should help the student notice when either the sequence of the story being narrated is muddled and/or if some of its details are distracting listeners from the main point. Again, this is another way to exercise those *sequential thinking muscles.*

Allowing children to narrate a story can sometimes cause certain problems that should be addressed before entering into this activity. Students tend to go on and on and on, leaving listeners bored. Have a time limit, set it preferably after conversation with your students, and adhere to it strictly so that everyone knows what to expect.

When students are reading their work, it is important to model the critical thinking skills necessary to help students become their own and each other's editors.

One by one, after students narrate their work, ask your class:

- What was the main theme of the author's story?
- How did the author support the main theme?
- Were there parts of the story whose purpose you didn't understand?
- Did the author seem to leave some parts out?

HELPFUL METAPHORS FOR SEQUENTIAL THINKING

We already talked about bridge building as a visual metaphor for sequential thinking. How about building a house with cards?

Try having students build a house with cards. The main idea is to consider the first floor as a foundation and subsequent floors as forms of elaboration. As the house (hopefully) becomes more elaborate, it is necessary that second and third floors be supported by the first floor, and yet it is also important that the second and third floors stay within the limits imposed by the strength of the first. Another way to demonstrate this concept is by putting toothpicks into marshmallows to create units that can be built into a structure. Through these activities students can see how every part of a structure is dependent upon the strength of another. No part of the structure, like no part of the story, proceeds by itself. A story of any kind needs a good foundation; one that will support elaboration that itself must not deviate too far from the central theme of the narrative. Or, what about setting up dominoes to fall into each other? Who can do the most? Why do some lines fall and others stop halfway through? What is being left out or not considered effectively?

CONNECTING WITH THE MAIN IDEA

Our work as teachers is to help students make the connections between the details of the story and the main ideas they are trying to convey. Writing a story can be like a jazz improvisation: There is a main theme and there are tributaries or improvisations that use elements of the main theme to explore and investigate other directions for the tune. For example, even as the musician takes us away from the main theme, you nonetheless have confidence that the musician retains the central theme and remains aware of the relationship between the improvisation and its main source. When you hear a few familiar notes or rhythms from the main theme, you are confident that you are going to be able to eventually get back to the main theme or tune. You are also often left feeling amazed that so many sub-themes can be generated from the main one. The path of a river is certainly another way to visualize this process; studying the river's flow on a map (or in person) is a good way to help students visualize and understand the relationship between subplots and the details to the main narrative.

Here is a list of activities where sequences and/or logical thinking play an integral part:

- Organize a scavenger hunt where each of the clues is a sentence in a story . . . a story that is finished when the hunt is completed.
- Organize a relay race. Divide your class into teams. The first person on each team must write a beginning sentence to a story on a clipboard and once complete must walk quickly to the next person on the team. The next person then writes a second sentence before bringing the clipboard to the next in line, and so forth. The game is complete when the last person in line writes the story's ending and finishes the last part of their "lap." Then the teams read their stories aloud, and the team that finishes first *with* a logically sequential story "wins."
- Play an old theater game where one person starts a movement and passes it on to the next person who then takes movement and transforms it into another, before passing that movement onto the following player.
- Play the telephone game. At the end, go over what each person told the other on their way to the inevitable misinterpretation at the end.
- Create a hopscotch game by placing words in each square. One by one ask students to jump from square to square and make a sentence. Write it down and see if it makes sense. The sentence each student creates must relate to the one before. See if you can get a story by the end.
- Have students give directions to their house.
- Write funny pieces that ignore important sequential events, like seasonal change, with a story about winter going directly into summer; chronological change, with someone going from birth to old age; or a meal where courses are eaten in the wrong order.

- Play the basketball game "Horse," where you take a shot that someone else has already made and then make a new one for the next in line to copy as well. The person who is able to remember and to make all of the shots from the previous players wins.
- Have students sell a product that has all logical claims except for one claim that the other students hopefully would be able to point out. For instance, a child selling a pair of sneakers claims that the shoes will help you to run faster than anyone in school. The child shows a video of some great athletes running a very fast 40 meters while wearing the same sneakers. The child says that if you wear those sneakers you will be able to run just as fast. Hopefully students will ask: "But, don't these runners have more natural talent than I do and haven't they practiced a great deal more? How do we know that it's the sneaker that makes them so fast?" Now, if instead of the athletes the child shows you a video of a regular kid first running slowly and then, after putting on the sneakers, running exceedingly fast, you might have something; but wait a minute, how do we know the kid was really trying the first time? It's like the "before" and "after" weight loss photos . . . which is really "before" and which is really "after"?
- For those who play music—even a simple recorder—play a composition or sing a song, cutting out the middle and going right from beginning to end.
- Create an autobiography.
- Make a timeline of someone's life.
- Have everyone in the class build something together, like a model airplane or a playhouse, or assemble a sound system. Follow written directions and if you want to have some fun, leave out one step when you are writing directions and see what happens and if someone notices.
- Have students describe a game of baseball, basketball, or football they participated in or a TV show or movie they viewed.
- Show a film to your students, but break it off in the middle and just go to the end.
- Take a story with quite a few pages, copy it, and give it out with the pages mixed up. Have groups of students put it together correctly.

Whenever you play any of the above games, reinforce the fact that your students are actually discovering how sequential thinking works.

USING THE ARTS AND PHYSICAL EDUCATION TO TEACH SEQUENCE

Speak with your art teacher, your physical education teacher, and your music teacher for other ideas that will demonstrate the logic of sequential thinking and the problems that arise when you neglect it. Certainly, dance steps and theater dialogue are important to do sequentially. Musical scales are also sequential. The more you can use the arts to reinforce what you are trying to teach, the clearer, stronger, and longer lasting your lessons will be.

Now that we've had the discussion about the "sequence" of our relationship (it wasn't so difficult was it?), it's time to learn how to help students accurately and interestingly describe the world in their now, hopefully, sequentially perfect narratives.

3

Observation, Description, and Colorful Language

Encouraging Sensitivity to Detail and Observational Intelligence

OK everybody, before we start this chapter, put the book down, turn the cell phones off, take a deep breath, close your eyes, and simply listen to your breath going in and out of your body because this chapter is about learning how to *pay attention.*

> When we complain that our students are not able to describe in detail, it is like asking someone who has been in bed for two years to bench press 300 pounds. The muscles just aren't there.

We take in a huge amount of detail every day, just by waking up, having breakfast, showering, putting on clothes, and going to work. Mostly, the details of everyday life are essentially backdrops for doing what we have to get done . . . the necessities. In some ways, ignoring the details of everyday life *is* necessary to get us from Point A to Point B. How many things can we notice if we're simultaneously driving the kids to school, thinking about work and preparing for a parental visit, and ruminating over an argument with our significant other. Our problem, as we become "grown-ups," is that life has become a series of goings and comings, of Point A's to Point B's and we forget, as the cliché goes, to smell the flowers . . . or the coffee . . . depending perhaps on the time of year and the choice of morning beverage. We are so fixated on getting done what needs to be done that we forget to pay attention to the journey . . . and to what is interesting by the side of the road.

Now I don't want to begin sounding like one of the many self-help or New Age books in the aisles of your favorite bookstore . . . not to say that I haven't read and benefited from my share. But I do want to point out that we are living in a world of *non-observation* . . . or in a *hurry-up* world: "Hurry up and get ready for school." "Hurry up and put on your soccer shoes." "Hurry up, it's time to take a shower and go to bed." "Hurry up and finish dinner."

In a hurry-up world, it is difficult to take time to either observe or describe. We don't give our children or ourselves the time to sit quietly, to look, notice, and observe. Every moment of our time and of much our children's time is filled like a program menu for satellite TV. Every moment is filled. Even for the many kids who don't have all kinds of adult-generated activities to distract them, they are busy watching TV or playing video games. How many of us or how many kids are just sitting quietly looking out the window at the rain falling down on a pane of glass, the snow drifting on a winter day, or a bird landing and taking a worm from the ground?

The first step toward encouraging good observation and description is to "build up the muscles," in order to promote what I call, *observational intelligence*. What is observational intelligence? Simply stated, it is the ability to consciously notice and then to describe what we are noticing: to notice and to articulate.

Tips for Teaching Observation

- Sit quietly, close your eyes, and listen to music. What instruments can you hear?
- Look at photos or pictures of paintings and talk about what you see.
- Sketch a still life, a park, a classroom, a person.
- Sit on a park bench.
- Bring in a number of things to smell and have students describe them.
- Do the same thing with tastes.
- Ask students to move around the classroom in slow motion.
- Look up at the clouds.
- Watch some bees gather pollen or ants crawl on the sidewalk.
- Have students take photos at the same intersection from the same angle every 15 minutes. The next day look at the pictures and notice the differences.

Tips for Teaching Description

- Look out the classroom window, go back to the desks, and have students describe in detail what they saw and heard.
- Observe the contents of the classroom and then ask students to close their eyes and describe what they saw, heard, and smelled.
- Take a walk around the block or to a park and have students write down what they saw, heard, and smelled.
- For a homework assignment, have students describe what they see and hear as they either go home from or to school.
- Have students describe their bedroom or living room or what they see out of one of the windows in their house.
- Have students describe the content of their refrigerators at home.
- Have students describe the outside of a house or an apartment building in detail.
- Have students describe a beach they've visited, a forest, or an overgrown lot. Again, what did they see, hear, and smell?
- Each day as students come in, ask them to describe how the sky looked that day.

A Little More Complicated . . .

- Have students describe the differences between two houses they've visited . . . ones belonging to two different friends or relatives.
- Have students describe visiting places at different times of the year or day . . . say, for instance, a park outside their house in both summer and fall, or an afterschool center or a supermarket when it is crowded and when it is empty.
- Ask students if they have ever revisited a house where they've lived or visited at different stages of their lives. If they have, ask them

describe how the house looked, smelled, and sounded differently at these different points. You can do this with an amusement park, a baseball field, a store, and so on.
- Have students describe how their houses change for different occasions: holidays, visitors, etc. Do the dishes change? Are there flowers around? Is the house cleaner? Is there music?
- Have students describe the food that was served at a holiday dinner.
- Have students describe a smell that evokes a memory of an occasion.
- Take students blindfolded into the cafeteria or out into the schoolyard and ask them to detail the sounds they hear and the smells they notice.

To describe the *outer* world is one thing; to describe the *inner* or emotional world is another. This is more difficult for young people. Without a lot of attention given either at home or in school to the language of feelings, it is difficult for students to know how to identify and describe their own or their character's emotional world. So in the same way, it is important to build the muscles for observing, noticing, and describing the *outer* world; we must do the same for the *inner* world.

The best way to have students pay attention to their psychological world is to first create a classroom that supports this kind of dialogue. If each day, students get to sit in a circle and discuss their last evening or weekend, we've gone a long way toward opening the door for the exchange and growth of an emotional vocabulary. You, as a teacher, will need to prompt these discussions with questions, especially as you begin this process: How did you feel when you fell off the bike? Were you happy to see your grandmother and grandfather? Were you disappointed that your father couldn't take you to the baseball game? By prompting students with questions, you will get them to think deeper about what they are describing.

IMPROVING QUESTION-ASKING SKILLS

I'm going to take a quick detour here into question asking, because I feel that *question asking* is one of the great tools for encouraging good descriptive writing.

Most people will not elaborate verbally unless asked. Most people "read" a lack of questions from a listener as a lack of interest. Most of us, if we sense that someone is not interested in something we have experienced and want to talk about, usually shut down. Why not? It's probably a healthy response, socially speaking. After all, we all know the person who talks and talks and talks and doesn't respond to your cues.

It is important that students feel what they say is of interest to you and others. *Active listening* is a popular phrase from a few years ago. When someone is talking, we should not only listen attentively, we need to ask questions that encourage the speaker to more fully elaborate about what they are communicating. For instance, if a student tells you about having to go to a grown-up party and how bored they were, ask them: "What kind of party was it?" "Who was there?" "What did the boredom *feel* like?" By asking this last question, it helps students pay more attention to how they express those feelings in their body . . . sweaty hands, dress too tight, feet feeling too big for their shoes. If a student talks about how long the drive was to the family's summer vacation, you might ask, "What they did to pass the time?" If they say they played games, you might ask, "What games?" If they tell you the names of the games, you might ask, "How is it played or did anything interesting happen when you were playing?"

By asking pointed questions, we become guides for our students, helping them to delve deeper into their experiences.

Learning to ask good questions is an art form. Ask any psychologist or, in fact, even Larry King. How do we ask questions in ways that help push the speaker to think beyond yes or no answers? How do we assess when the person questioned is withholding information simply because they need help in understanding how to give a more elaborate answer? How do we help them to articulate a more complete answer? How do we use one answer to stimulate the next question?

Good question asking involves learning how to *pay attention*.

When we *really* listening to someone tell a story or narrate an incident, we try not to judge. Instead, we listen for the narrative and the gaps in their "story." We try, as much as possible, to keep ourselves "out" of the narrative, except as facilitators. Ask yourself and help your students to ask while listening to someone tell their story, what is being glossed over? What emotions and feelings are being masked when they say, "I felt bad" "I felt bored" "I was frustrated."

When asking questions yourself and teaching students to ask questions, the key word is *elaboration*. How do we encourage people to elaborate in their stories? One way is to use words like *how* and *why*. Or phrases like:

"What do you mean by that?"

"Can you describe more about what you are saying?"

"How did you feel when that happened?"

"Why do you think such and such happened the way it did?"

These are simple phrases that you and your students can use when listening and trying to "draw out" storytellers to help them elaborate, to expand like an accordion, to look beneath the tip of the iceberg.

To help students not to hide behind words that are too vague (for example, nervous, cute, weird) when they are asked questions about how they feel or what they have experienced, remind them to "go down into their bodies" and to not just "name" the feeling, but to describe how that feeling affected their "insides." Students will often say, "I don't remember" or will look uncomfortable when asked to "get deeper" but keep persisting (up to a point), because kids remember a lot more than they initially let on. They just need to be prompted and given the confidence that they can "go there" and that someone really cares about what they have to say. By encouraging students in this way to observe and describe both the *inside* and *outside* worlds, we are helping them to elaborate and to ultimately create metaphors and similes in order to *show* and not just *tell*. More on this later . . .

Teaching for *Deep Questioning*

- Conducting oral histories with parents or peers is a good way to help students work on *their* question-asking skills. Taking the answers and creating biographies or memoirs will help students see how important good question asking (and detail gathering) is. Taking those biographies, reading them to the class, and asking the class to identify what information is missing is a good way to reinforce the importance of critical thinking, details, and sequence. "What questions could have been asked to get that information?" is an important question *you* can ask as you go over the biographies or memoirs.
- Another way to help stimulate your students' facility for question asking is to create a student newspaper, radio program, or TV show. Students become the reporters and editors, and they find and report about what is going on in classrooms or a Little League game, or a class field trip. Here again, they must ask questions and construct stories while students, as editors, need to listen to the stories with an ear to seeing what gaps needed to be filled and by what questions.
- Third, ask students to role play different vocations where question asking is important: detective, investigative reporter, doctor, or a mechanic trying to figure out what's wrong with a car. What questions should they ask? How should they use answers to stimulate new questions? How should they form follow-up questions that will lead to more than one-word answers?

Remember that you, as the teacher, are the main role model for question asking and are ultimately responsible for helping students "dig deeper" into their experiences and emotions. When you help students become good *question askers*, you help them to look at their own work more critically.

FROM QUESTIONS TO COLORFUL LANGUAGE . . . THEN BACK TO DESCRIPTION

Take a few emotionally charged words—sad, lonely, happy, confused, angry, and embarrassed—and ask your students if they have ever felt these emotions. If the answer is "yes," ask them when and under what circumstances. An important next question to help your students "go deeper" and to identify colorful, descriptive language is to ask how these emotional states "felt" in the body. *This point is key.*

> If we ask the right questions and help students to identify emotions, we are on the right road, but if we can help students identify *how* those emotions actually expressed themselves in the body and mind, we have good raw material for elaborative, identifying, and colorful language.

Let's take *confusion*. "No, you take confusion, I have too much of my own," you are probably thinking. That said, what *does* confusion really feel like? Your stomach churns, your head feels filled up to the point of distraction, and you are emotionally and, at times, physically paralyzed. For example, what is there in the world that we or the students have seen or experienced that churns: a blender, an ice cream maker, your stomach after an amusement park ride? What is filled up to the point of distraction: a newspaper, a phone book, the morning fog at the beach? What can't move: a telephone pole?

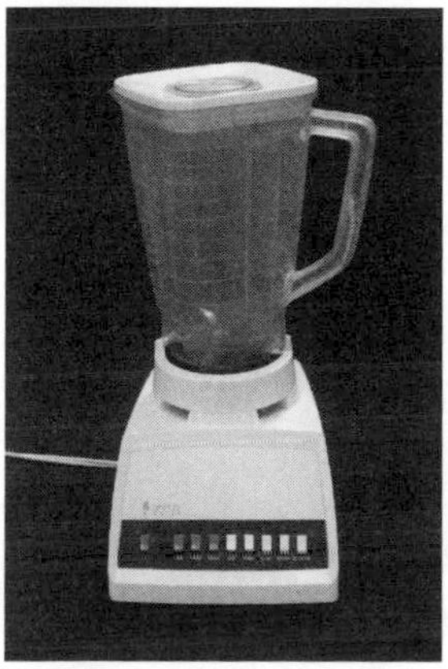

From naming the emotion or feeling, we go to the body to see how that feeling manifests itself, from the body to something in the world that can be compared to that feeling and from that something in the world to metaphor and simile. We create our metaphors and similes by connecting what we see, hear, feel, and taste to something in the world we've noticed. This is where all the time you've devoted to teaching *observational intelligence* pays off.

HELPING STUDENTS CREATE METAPHORS AND SIMILES

An activity that I like to use to help students think metaphorically is . . . drumroll please . . . "the Metaphor and Simile Olympics." Two teams of three students each stand in the front of the room and I start by saying something like, "I feel so cold I feel like . . ." (fill in the blank). One team at a time has to finish this sentence differently until one team is unable to find yet another metaphor or simile (I still have difficulty telling the difference between metaphor and simile . . . whoops, maybe I shouldn't let that out), and the other team "wins" and continues to play against another group of students. The opportunities are endless. I feel so cold, so scared, so excited, so happy, so sad, and so angry. I shivered like a . . . . Her voice was so horrible it sounded like . . . . He was so tall he was like a . . . . The lines in her face looked like . . . . The snow fell on the hill like a . . . . He stood alone like a . . . . You get the idea.

When I play this game, I often have to help, especially initially. OK, what does it feel like when you are angry? What does your body feel like? Tense? OK, tight, hmm . . . ready to explode? Good. What explodes? Firecracker, that's good. Bomb, balloon, OK, nice job!

> Finding good metaphors and similes is a question of having experiences, *really* paying attention to those experiences, and having the time and attention to turn those experiences into descriptive phrases.

What kind of experiences do your students have that can be used to create metaphors and similes?

- We've felt the hot muggy heat on a summer day in a city.
- We've all looked at lonely weed-filled lots on the dividing lines between city and suburbs.
- We've heard a police siren scream in the middle of the night.
- We've watched lightning bugs blink haphazardly on a summer evening.
- We've smelled garbage piling up.
- We've experienced the arrival of a storm as the sky darkens.

Student experiences of what they've seen, heard, smelled, tasted, and felt fills an important section of our students' writer's toolbox. Always find ways to encourage your students to describe new experiences and observations. Look through photographic and art books to help them notice unusual things. The more they notice; the more unusual and idiosyncratic; the more their writing will reflect who they uniquely are. Haven't we all read wonderful poetry or fiction and just been completely jolted by unexpected metaphors and similes? "Where did that come from?"

> Finding colorful and metaphoric language is not unlike any artistic process. It is the combination of hard work and magic.

The magic happens when the "dots are connecting" or where the "synapses are firing." For example, a writer describes loneliness as being like the last leaf on a late autumn tree or the exhilaration a character feels is not unlike the early spring evening sounds of peeper frogs celebrating the warming of the earth. For the magic to happen, we must create the space to recall and have the confidence that the connections will be made. Students need to understand that everything they've seen, heard, tasted, smelled, and felt can be used in their writing to help communicate to others their own or a character's emotional experiences.

Here's another activity: Provide two columns of words and phrases. Have the students match one column to another and then explain why they've chosen to link the two.

1. When my father is angry, he is like a	a. Leaf thrown floating on a river
2. My grandfather's face is like a	b. The streaks of rain on a car window
3. When we won the game, I was so happy I felt like a	c. There are stars in the sky
4. When I was lost, I felt like a	d. A road map of the United States
5. The sun was warm with the memory of	e. Summer
6. Sitting in church all dressed up on a hot summer morning, I felt like	f. Overcooked noodles
7. The graffiti on the wall of the school looked like	g. Cooked hot dog in a steamy bun
8. By the end of the day, I felt so tired my body felt like a	h. Mother bear protecting her cub
9. I cried as many tears as	i. Child alone in a candy store

Another fun exercise is trying to create metaphors and similes that are opposite to what you are trying to describe. You know, "After the bath, I was so clean I looked like a baseball player's uniform after they played a double header in the rain." Or, "When I heard that there was a present waiting for me at home, I ran as fast as the grass grows." This exercise is kind of like the card game, "Give-Away," which is the opposite of the card game called "War." In one, you are trying to get as many of the opponent's cards as you can while in the other, you are trying to give them all of yours. By doing the opposite of what you are trying to do, you can develop a better understanding of what your goal actually is . . . and in a fun way.

KEEPING IT FUN IN A NURTURING AND JOYFUL ENVIRONMENT

That moment we talked about when the perfect metaphor or simile comes to you is a magic moment . . . a mini-epiphany . . . a small "peak experience." Students need to feel what this feels like so they can recognize it again and again. It is a form of problem solving, and like I said, not unlike any creative activity.

The more opportunities you can provide for students where they can successfully solve a problem, the more familiar they will be with the state of mind they need to keep revisiting. The more success they have in solving problems (in art, music, science, math, construction, theater . . . anything), the more confidence they will have in coping with the momentary frustrations that come in the beginning of any new challenge. Students, in fact all of us, need to develop the faith and patience to confidently sit quietly for a moment or more while the synapses are firing away and before the numbers flash on the "calculator's screen." We need to trust that we can depend on those *organizing* moments for the brain to scan its *database* in order to *unpack* the visceral elements of what we want to describe and to then find its appropriate metaphor or simile.

Finding metaphors and similes is not unlike solving an algebraic equation. You are looking to find the common denominator between two experiences.

So, now that your students know *how* to describe . . . *who* do they want to describe . . . and just as importantly . . . *why*?

4

Finding and Using Characters

Using What You Know to Create Memorable Characters

Which family members do you recollect from family gatherings? Does anybody "stand out" from your neighborhood memories? How about among your ex-schoolmates or colleagues? I'm asking this to remind you that we all live within a social context. The people we see on our walks, in our stores, at our places of business, in our families, at our celebrations, at our religious rituals, and so on, all are part of our social context.

Your students are part of a social context as well. Why do I mention this? Why mention something so obvious? Because we tend to forget that students have their own circles of relatives, friends, and acquaintances to influence their writing. Our job in this chapter is to help you help them be aware of this so that creating characters for their stories and essays doesn't seem to be as mysterious and difficult as it often seems.

How do we do this?

First, have students simply think about the people in their lives.

Start with their immediate family . . . parents, siblings. Go to uncles, aunts, cousins, grandparents, parent's good friends. Next, look at neighbors. After that, include their friends, teachers, counselors, coaches, and religious leaders. Then, how about people they see in their local stores or notice just by chance on the street.

That's *a lot* of people.

Ask students to talk about one or more of these people. You might want to narrow down the number by choosing one of the above categories. Ask them to describe what the person looks like. Help them to remember the details of the person's face, eyes, hair color, body build, and so on.

FOCUSING ON LOOKS

A quick exercise to stimulate your students' ability to describe how someone physically appears is to ask them to pretend that after the first day of school their parents ask them to describe their new teacher. What would they say? How would they describe you?

Tell them not to be embarrassed if they giggle at first when describing you as "old." (I've been described that way many times.) Ask them what they mean and help them "unpack" that idea. (For more about *question asking*, see Chapter 3.) For example, "I have gray hair . . . ." You might ask: What kind of gray is it? What does it look like in the world that you know about . . . maybe gray like the sidewalk?

Don't let them get away with flattery (however tempting it is). "I'm pretty?" What does that mean? "Well, you have pretty hair," they might say. "What do you like about it?" you ask. "Its color," they reply. You: "How would you describe its color?" "Brown," they add. "Hmmm, brown like what: the bark of a tree or a chocolate bar?" you prompt.

OK, let's go back to *observation* for a minute. "Your hair is brown and your skin is black."

DISTINGUISHING BETWEEN SHADES OF COLORS

Have students make a list of all things "brown" that they've seen. Do the same thing for black and yellow, white and any other color you hear in the course of the descriptions. Blue and green always come up when describing eyes and since I have blue eyes, I always ask what kind of blue do they mean? When they say, "like the ocean" I try to ask the next question, which is: "The ocean on what kind of day?"

Too often students will stop at clichés. "Blue eyes like the ocean." Some educators would say that a description like that is fine, especially if the child is very young, but for me it is important to encourage subtle understanding as early as possible. It is in those subtle details that students can start to link personality and physical characteristics. For instance, "Blue eyes change like their personality does, sometimes calm and clear like the ocean at rest, sometimes blue-grey like the ocean in turbulence."

The color white used when describing skin color is another problem that needs quick attention. When someone says "white" as a skin color, it needs to be looked at more carefully. "You have white skin," students will sometimes say to me. Picking up a piece of white-lined paper and holding it next to my face is usually sufficient to create a distinction between the two. The inside of a peach usually becomes (correctly) the next description that students use.

Things to Do

- Create a wall chart naming different colors: brown, blue, yellow, etc. Under the colors have students add the names of objects that correspond to the color. In addition, make room on the chart so that not only can they add the name of the object but its picture if they can find one in a magazine or a catalogue.
- Have students draw a picture of their neighbor in class and then let the "model" become the "artist." By giving students the time to sit and look at someone, they will notice nuances in color and shape. Give them as many paints or crayons that you can find so that they will be able to make subtle color distinctions. To extend this activity, take a walk around the school building and have students select someone to sketch. Have the students do this activity at home as well.
- Have students look around the room and in their minds pick one student they want to describe. Have them write a description of that student on a piece of paper. The description of the student should only be of the student's face, no body and no clothes. For instance . . .

- o What shape is the face?
- o What shape and color are the eyes?
- o What about lines in the face?
- o What color is the hair?
- o What does the jaw, chin, and hairstyle look like?

Have students describe the colors and shapes as metaphorically as possible. Tell them *no* insults or descriptions that can be interpreted that way. In addition, don't let the students include easily identifiable items such as jewelry or glasses. This exercise is just about facial features and hair. Have students read their descriptions and have the class see if they can figure out who the student is. Give them three chances. If after the third try they still haven't figured out the "described student," the writer has to come up with a more detailed description.

DESCRIBING BEHAVIOR

Now that we have helped students describe a person's physical features, how about what the person is like and how the person behaves? All students understand the importance of a character's behavior to a work of fiction. After all, what would Cinderella be without the behavior of the three "wicked" stepsisters?

"They are funny," a student might say when asked about a cousin. Again, we need you to prompt: "Funny in what way?" "They have a nice personality," The student might reply. You: "What does that mean?" The student: "They are kind." You: "Can you give me examples? You think they are nice . . . what does nice mean to you? Do they help you make things? What kind of things? Do they talk with you and ask you questions? Have you seen them with others? What are they like with other people?"

> We help students to look, to notice, and to describe; that is, to develop *observational intelligence* and then to figure out how to use those people as characters in their stories.

NAILING DOWN THE DETAILS

When I was young, I watched the people at the local stores, my parent's friends, and the older kids in the neighborhood. I still can describe how Mr. Zimmerman, the man who owned the butcher shop, looked and behaved as well as the number from Auschwitz tattooed on his wrist. I was very aware of the candy store next to the tuxedo shop where Mr. Barenburg, a small, unhappy man, reluctantly dispensed Cherry

Cokes and long thin pretzels. I noticed the older kids, "Stevens" and "Burger" (I don't remember their first names because the older kids all called each other by last names), pick on Ronnie Gutman, who most of the time tried to defuse their taunts with self-deprecating laughter, but who when the teasing was too vicious would start to cry and run home. Or, speaking of Gutman, I remember when everyone found out that his father had just passed away and a solemn meeting of about 20 kids in the neighborhood all agreed to not pick on him . . . at least for a while.

This kind of memory for the details of people's behavior is not that unusual. Most kids have it. They live life being very aware of living within many communities of people where they are continually reassessing expectations, safety, and opportunities for fun. They are in a continuous dialogue with the social environment.

For instance, I was in the local newspaper and magazine store the other day and a young boy in a baseball team jersey, maybe 10 years old, was ahead of me in line ready to pay for about three types of candies. I can't recall the names of the candies, but he bought them and was walking out of the store, when suddenly he realized that he needed one more candy bar. I was paying for my newspaper as he waited to pay for his next piece of candy, when I said to him, in the mock adult style of admonition, "More candy?" He looked at me at first surprised that an adult should spontaneously start to talk with him. Then he quickly tried to figure out whether or not I was really criticizing his food purchasing habits, and when he finally realized that I was just joking with him, his face lit up in a smile and he joined the fun by saying, "I'm out of school and celebrating!" That young boy watched me for clues and when he thought that I was "safe" and uncritical, he responded. I'm sure that had I been his teacher asking him to write about that encounter, he could have described my behavior and his behavior in a lot more detail than I just did.

Again, students notice, they assess, they figure out. It is our job to get what's in their heads out on paper.

NOTICING AND DESCRIBING PEOPLE'S BEHAVIOR

Take many of the words that are used to describe how people behave and make a chart of them: weird, nice, greedy, funny, cheap, and angry, for instance. Have students write down examples of people behaving in each of these ways. These examples can come either directly from their lives or from books, video games, TV, or the movies. If they find pictures in magazines and the comics or comic books, then add these as well.

It is also important to leave space for students to recognize and describe people's seemingly contradictory behavior as well. After all, we've all seen a normally loving person act momentarily angry or a usually generous person act as if it was their last cent. While getting only as nuanced as you think students can, we need to call their attention to this more subtle point because it will lead ultimately to more interesting characters.

- Have students describe the times when they have felt or acted in two different ways with the same person. Help them to consider, for instance, how they have behaved with their siblings or with their parents.
- Have students think about how other people have behaved in their presence. Have they ever noticed people exhibiting different "sides" of themselves? What "triggered" that "mixed" behavior?
- Take a favorite folktale and have a main character act differently than usual . . . the "evil" Snow White, for instance. Write down how the other characters might act in these newly created situations.

USING FOLKTALES AND THE MASS MEDIA

The use of folktales and myths is a great way to study and help your students become more aware of how people behave. Certainly there are many examples of "black and white" behavior. The "wicked" stepsisters in *Cinderella*, the witch in *Hansel and Gretel*, the kindness of Snow White are just a few examples. Anansi the spider and Wylie Coyote are often full of guile. Jack of *Jack and the Beanstalk* fame often succeeds in spite of himself. Hadja, or (as he is sometimes called) Nasurdin, is a folk character from the Middle East who in spite of his seeming simplicity is often very wise. Seemingly contradictory behavior can be found in Greek and Hindu mythology where human and divine traits are often combined.

Cartoon and comic strips are also good resources for archetypes . . . Bluto in *Popeye* as the bully; Superman as the nerd who is secretly a superhero; Tom and Jerry, two characters who are constantly battling, yet are dependent on each other to determine who they are (remind you of certain marriages?); *Peanuts* with the often spacey, yet thoughtful Charlie Brown, the insecure Linus, and the bossy Lucy. And what can you say about Homer Simpson?

The list can go on and on. Conversations that analyze behavior in various media should go on every day. Once you've read or told a story, have a conversation about a character in that story by asking: "Do you know anyone like the characters in this comic, folktale, video game, etc? Do you know anyone who shares certain personality qualities with the characters we just learned about? How do they show who they are . . . through their behavior? Through the way they look? What do you mean by that?" Again, these conversations are part of building *observational intelligence* in your classroom and in your students *noticing . . . observing . . . describing*!

OBSERVING HOW BODIES MOVE

Now that we have talked about physical and psychological description, we need to help students notice and describe the body's movements and gestures: how someone walks, sits, lies down, looks around, etc., and at how that behavior helps to reveal that person's personality. What are some physical cues that signal certain types of moods, behavior, or personalities? How do people walk when they are confident? How do they walk when they are tired? How about when they are sad or when they are immersed in their own thoughts. Why is a "poker face" called a poker face?

- Take students on a walk outside of school and have them simply watch people on the street. Let them speculate about the people they notice. "How is that person feeling? Where do you think they are going or coming from? What do you think they are like?" Have your students justify their speculation by referring to how the person is moving, standing, or sitting.
- The world of painting and sculpture is filled with examples of artists trying to share their understanding of a subject's psychology. From Gothic depictions of a mother's love; to Renaissance paintings of veneration, ecstasy, and sadness; through Flemish paintings of the newly confident professional class; through Rodin's *The Thinker*, Munch's *The Scream*, and Hopper's emotionally ambiguous paintings of individuals alone in the then "modern" world, we can see how artists have brought us into the personalities and emotions of their subjects. By looking at these and other artists' works, we can help students notice how artists depict their subjects in ways that help us understand who that person is and what they are feeling. How are they walking? Erect and confident or stooped like they are carrying the weight of the world's problems? What are they doing with their hands or arms? What kind of look is in their eyes? Ask students to look at paintings and sculptures and speculate on the personalities of the subject, giving reasons for their speculation. This helps them to notice and describe how the physical reveals the psychological.
- Get students out of their seats and suggest emotions for them to display using only their bodies. No words! For example, *anger*. Let them first strike a pose of anger and then move around the room with that anger inside. When you finish, have a discussion of how their bodies felt during this exercise. What parts of their bodies were tense? What parts felt relaxed? Have the others in the class, the audience in this case, do the same for the child who was acting.
- Have students secretly choose an emotion they want to display to the class and see if the others can guess it. When they do guess correctly, have the students discuss what in the student's stance or movement gave away the personality or emotion.

- Listen to music: symphonies, jazz, contemporary. Ask students how the music makes them feel. If they can (and I know that not all kids will do this . . . but don't push it), have them move around the room in the way the music makes their bodies feel. Talk about the ways in which their body parts were working.

HARNESSING THE INTERNAL MONOLOGUE

A word or two about how we all talk to ourselves:

The conversations that people have with themselves, the voices that go on in our heads as we plan, remember, worry, resent, and so on are important parts of who we are. The internal monologue can shed light on a character's motivation and how they see themselves. While many say we are overburdened with a cacophony of thoughts, nonetheless they *are* a part of who we are. As your students depict characters, they need to be aware of how to make their character's internal monologue visible.

Students, depending on their ages and development, all have internal monologue. They are thinking, plotting, and deciding. For instance, when I was six years old and in first grade, I had a crush on a girl named Susan, "all the way" back from kindergarten. I considered how to stand in back of her on the dance line, waited across the street from a house in my neighborhood where I knew she was visiting, and even went to her house for a "tea" party. We liked each other. Then in first grade, a friend had a party and toward the end of the party, Susan began to chase me out the apartment and up the stairs until we could go no further. In a fit of eloquence that I have never been able to duplicate, I said, "'Now that you got me, what do you want to do with me?" She then gave me a kiss on the cheek and left me floating down the stairs and back into the apartment where my mother was waiting to take me home. When I got into the car, my father and brother were there and, full of excitement about this new and wonderful experience, I told them all what had happened. To my surprise and disappointment, everyone started to laugh. At that moment, I told myself that they were not going to know anything else about my personal life . . . and they didn't.

This is an interesting story in itself (I feel anyway), but I told it because I wanted to demonstrate that at an early age, children are thinking and have a sense of the "thinker" inside.

Helping Students Locate and Express Internal Monologue

- Simply have students be quiet and listen to their voice inside. After five minutes of this, have them write down what they are thinking. Tell students that there is no right or wrong nor bad or good here and that students will not be forced to share what they are thinking about to anyone else.

- Again, take students outside and have them notice one person and write down what they think that person is thinking. Ask them why they speculated the way they did.
- Find a good book of photographic portraits . . . Walker Evans, Jacob Riis, Arthur Penn, Richard Avedon, or some sort of compilation or collection and have students pick out a person photographed. Have them write an internal monologue for that person. Do the same with pictures you find in the daily newspaper and/or with comic book characters.
- Look at cartoon and comic strips and notice how the "thought bubble" is used to make the internal monologue visible. Those of you who want to be more "sophisticated" might want to look at some Roy Lichtenstein paintings where he takes comic strips and blows them up, giving a lot of attention to frames with "thought bubbles."
- Have students take a character out a folktale or fairy tale and write an internal monologue for them.
- Write down some *age-appropriate* situations your students might find themselves in. These might include: sitting all dressed up in church, synagogue, temple, or mosque on a hot day; meeting your father's new girl friend; getting ready for summer camp; packing for a move to a new city; and bringing home a "bad" report card. Put these suggestions into a hat and have students select one and write the monologue they imagine might be in someone's head in the situation they've selected.

THE ROLE OF CHARACTERS IN CREATING STORIES

Imagine "Rip Van Winkle" without Rip Van Winkle or the Headless Horseman without . . . well, you get the point. People *are* the story. Most of the time, the story is about people. These examples are extremes because in both cases the travails of the character I "removed" were what the story is about. Think of Sancho Panza in *Don Quixote,* Robin in the *Batman and Robin* comics, and Watson in the Sherlock Holmes novels. These are not main characters, but their presence is important for moving the story along, creating conflicts, and helping the main characters define themselves. Villains, helpers, and fellow travelers all serve a role in creating a narrative whole. Think of the *Wizard of Oz*. Each character has a specific role without which the story would have less color. Who is the hero? Who is the foil? Who encourages the hero? Who presents obstacles to the hero? Who is the bully to the "nerd" and creates an opportunity for the hero to be a hero? Who is leader of a group of girls who band together against someone new? Which girl refuses to go along and befriends the new girl?

How do we get students to look at, understand, and use subsidiary characters that will help them to move the narrative along? Again, I start at the roots . . . their own lives. Who are the people who have influenced them, changed them, created roadblocks or helped them through difficult situations.

- Have students create a board game based on their lives, called Helpers and Hinderers. They should begin at birth and end . . . well, at "happiness." At various points in the game have students create places to land named after people who either helped or hindered the game's creator. When someone playing the game arrives on a Helper space, they advance the number of spaces the game's creator feels is appropriate for the help they've been given. If they land on a Hinderer space, they go backward a certain number of spaces depending on the game's architect's idea of how much that person has made their lives difficult. For instance, you are moving along the board and you land on "Uncle Jack" and it says, "Uncle Jack taught me how to throw a football. Move forward two spaces." Or you land on "Johnny Hill" and it says, "Johnny Hill was a bully who threw me into the bushes. Go back three spaces." Helpers and Hinderers could be relatives, teachers, coaches, neighbors, bullies; the list goes on. Having the older students create a few places where someone was hindering them actually taught them a valuable lesson. For instance you land on "Mrs. Kubek, Grade 5 teacher" and it says, "Mrs. Kubek was very strict and yelled at me for poor spelling, but she made me work harder. Move forward three spaces." Make time not only to create and play these games, but allot time for students to talk and write about how each of the helpers or hinderers either helped or hindered them.
- Have students write about a sports event they were part of. Have them talk about the various players and what they contributed to the game, either positively or negatively. For instance, someone made an error or hit a home run, scored a goal, or made an assist. Have them watch a game on TV and do the same for that game. By doing this, students become aware of the role each person serves in various social settings and ultimately they will have a better understanding of how to introduce characters into their stories to fill certain functions.
- Have students describe a family party. What is the "role" of each individual? Which people are cooking, cleaning, serving? Who is making people laugh? Who is getting into trouble?

Looking at Characters in Literature and Mass Media

- Have students look at the characters in their favorite TV show and ask them to delineate the role each person plays in that ensemble. Do the same with a comic strip, novel, or a movie. For instance, who is the understanding one, the one who is always saying something inappropriate, the one who is observing and commenting on an action, or the one who solves the crimes?

- If you can find them, watch DVDs of old TV shows of comedy teams: Abbott and Costello, Laurel and Hardy, Smothers Brothers, Sonny and Cher, and Marx Brothers and have students look at and analyze the role each member of the comedy team is playing.

DEALING WITH DIALOGUE

Creating characters is not only about showing how someone looks, dresses, or thinks to themselves, it is also about how they interact with the world . . . in this case, with other people. This includes both verbal and nonverbal interaction. A dialogue between two people reveals who those people are, at least in the context of that particular interaction. As most students know, how you talk depends on who you are talking with and the purpose for your conversation. How you talk with your parents differs from conversations with your peers. You talk with a teacher differently than you speak with a baby brother or sister. While students know this, many have, I'm sure, been reprimanded for talking with disrespect to an adult without realizing they were letting one conversational style bleed inappropriately into another type of relationship. Before you deal with dialogue, help to make students aware of how they (most of the time) speak to different people in different ways and often with different intentions in mind.

For instance, have them look at how they would greet different people. How do they say hello to their grandmother, their teacher, their friend? How do they talk to their parents if all they want to do is to go into their room and play a video game, versus speaking with them when you want your allowance increased? How do they talk with a younger sibling when their younger sibling is pestering them to play together, versus when they need the same sibling to keep a secret?

> Once you get students to realize how conversation is "site specific," have them play with various roles and conversational styles.

- Set up a number of age appropriate situations for students to role-play in pairs. Students can help to brainstorm these. Examples include parents lecturing a child about coming home late, younger siblings wanting to go shopping with older siblings, and children trying to convince their teenage babysitter to let them stay up later than their bedtime. Now have the students set up their own situations similar to the ones above and write dialogue for this newly created interaction.

- Become more specific about the types of situations you want to explore emotionally. For instance, create two characters conspiring about something; two characters arguing about something; two characters bargaining with each other; two characters playing something together; or two characters at a dance, where one is trying to get to know the other (for older students). Have students write the dialogue.
- Explore how characters would talk when various feelings are involved . . . embarrassment, bragging, guilty, happy, cautious, and so on. Find situations where these ways of talking can be explored in a dialogue.
- Have students write dialogue where one person speaks inappropriately to another . . . No cursing!
- Create environments where dialogues can happen, and have students explore the possible conversations . . . a stuck elevator, sitting in the office with another student waiting to speak with the principal, meeting your mother's new boyfriend.

USING OBJECTS AND DRESS TO CREATE CHARACTERS

Clothes

We choose the clothes we wear for a variety of reasons. Sometimes we put on anything as we work in the garden, take out the garbage, or read the Sunday paper. Most of the time, however, we choose clothes for a specific purpose: to impress at a job interview, to show how young we look, to make ourselves attractive, to go "out on the town." Of course we all know, especially if you've been around children or if you remember your days as a child, that the "right" clothes are exceptionally important.

When I was around eight years old, I began to notice how people were dressed and, of course, became fascinated with the clothes of the "tough" kids—tight black pants, T-shirts, leather jackets, or pastel-colored sports jackets with skinny ties. I had very strict ideas about what I would and wouldn't wear from an early age. The way I rolled up my short-sleeved shirts to how tight I wore my pants was closely considered and hotly debated within my family. What I could and couldn't wear was always a site for controversy. I suspect the same was true for many of you.

As students create characters, they need to notice that what a person wears can be a "giveaway" to a part of who they are, who they pretend to be, or what they aspire to be. Clothes often are the way people symbolically join a "club" . . . the football jersey, the Hermes bag, the baggy clothes of Hip Hop, or the loose fitting pants of skateboarders. Revealing certain places on the body is also a decision that puts the "wearer" inside a group . . . for instance, the belly-revealing shirts of today's teenage girls or a weight lifter's tight T-shirt. As students "draw" characters, it is important that they include clothing choice as part of the equation.

Helping Students Notice and Describe How People Dress

- Tell students a quick story about what clothes meant to you when you were younger.
- Have students tell you (and later have them write down) the different types of clothing their peers wear and describe how those clothes signify one group or another . . . prep, skater, Goth, etc.
- Have students talk about how they make their decisions about what to wear. What are the various thoughts they have when they are picking out clothes for different occasions . . . school, party, family gatherings?
- Have students describe conflicts they've had with their parents about the clothes, tattoos, body piercing, jewelry, hairstyle, or makeup they want to wear.
- How do your students buy clothes? Who do they go with? Where do they go? What do they think about? Where do they get the money?
- Where do your students get ideas for what to wear? Celebrities? Other kids? Stores? Ads?
- How do your students feel when their parents or other relatives buy them clothes?
- Have students consider how they feel in different types of clothes. Do these clothes make them walk in a certain way? Do they feel confident? Feel like a "baby"? Feel all grown up? Feel "uptight"? Feel cool? How do their clothes help them to walk, talk, and stand differently?

- Have students study people on the street. By looking at their clothes, can students speculate about the people they see? Who they are? What they are like?

THE ROLE OF INANIMATE OBJECTS

What child (or adult, for that matter) doesn't still have a toy, blanket, shirt, etc., from another stage of their lives? What does that object tell about who we were or are? For me, early important possessions in my life were the football my father gave me when I was born, the toy soldiers I would play with on the floor of my bedroom, my baseball cards and baseball glove, and later my record player and radio.

Objects or possessions play an important part in people's lives. We think a lot about the objects we want surrounding us. Many adults consider a house and car as very important for their self-esteem and identity. It's important to understand the objects that a person attaches to, hoards, and identifies with when creating a character; for example, the person who has years worth of old cars in various states of repair and disrepair in their front yard, the elderly woman and her window boxes filled with geraniums, the elderly man and his one bowling league trophy on the mantel place, the family photos in someone's house, someone's lucky charm, a young man's MP3 player. Think of characters on TV, in comic books, and in literature and how they were more clearly articulated with the help of "props" . . . Kojak's lollipop, Sherlock Holmes's pipe, Linus's blanket.

> We get attached to objects and in a funny way are in conversation with them. They give us security, provide a connection with the past, and reveal certain eccentricities. By including attachment to personal objects in the creation of a character, students make that character's uniqueness stand out.

Understand the Role of Personal Objects in People's Lives

- Tell students about objects that you connected to as a child, as well as any objects that have contemporary significance for you. Are there any objects from childhood that you still have? Bring them in.
- Have students talk about the objects that are important to them. Where did they get them? Why are they important?
- Ask students if their parents ever threw away objects that were important to them? For me, it was my baseball cards and to this day . . . tragic!
- Learn a bit about what the upper classes in Egypt put into their tombs as objects for the journey into the "afterworld." Have

students ask their parents or grandparents what objects they took with them when they moved from another house, from one state to another, or from another country to the United States. Have students take a photograph of the object, bring it in, or draw a picture of it and tell why their parents considered it so important.

- Ask students to notice what their neighbors do with their possessions. Do some have neighbors who are always polishing their cars, working on the yard, fixing bicycles, or building fences?
- What about animals? Do students notice their neighbors walking their dogs? Is there anything funny about the way people relate to their animals that gives you a sense of who they are?
- Ask students if they have ever noticed grown-ups who are not as adept with modern technology as they are? How about their mother wrestling with an MP3 player or their grandfather trying to understand his new cell phone. How a person relates successfully or unsuccessfully to technology is another interesting and telling detail when you are describing who they are. Have students think about and identify two people, one who relates well to technology and one who doesn't. Does the one who doesn't "get" technology become frustrated when they interact with it?

CREATING CHARACTERS AS A COLLAGE

OK, we've looked at how faces, bodies, dress, personal possessions, monologues, and dialogues give us a sense of who someone is. Now it is time to help students put all those attributes together. Some characters are taken "full cloth" from people an author has met . . . cut and pasted, if you will. Others are composites, combinations of various attributes that they've seen, thought about, learned about in books, movies, conversations, or other sources. It is these characters and how to teach their creation that I want to look at.

> Creating characters for stories is like creating a collage; you pick and choose parts of one person and graft it to parts of another real or fictional person.

Let's say you are trying to describe a bully . . . maybe a bully with some sensitivity and a character you want the readers to show some sympathy for. You might start by thinking of some of the physical characteristics of people who have intimidated or frightened you. Certainly for a bully, you might exaggerate certain features, at least if you were initially describing them from the point of view of someone who was the bully's victim. Maybe it's the size you would create first . . . the size of the body, head, arms, hands. Maybe there was something about the bully's veins head that protruded in a certain way when he was about to strike. Maybe it was the kind of shirts he wore, with sleeves rolled up that revealed muscles or even a tattoo. Maybe this bully had a disdainful smile when he teased you, but perhaps you saw the bully gently pet a cat that came his way and all of a sudden your idea of the bully changed.

Where did these ideas come from? Where did the idea for the veins come from, for instance? Maybe you saw them on your father when he got angry with you for asking one too many times for permission to stay up to watch a program. Perhaps the arm revealing a tattoo came from some guy you saw at the bowling alley. Maybe the sneer came from a character in the movie you saw, and the sensitivity for cats comes from your own liking of those animals.

All authors borrow and combine when they are creating fiction. Often it is the mole on the neck taken from one person that's added to the otherwise unblemished skin of a heroine that gives that person their humanness.

> Characters do not have to come into fiction wholly intact. Students need to understand that when they are writing fiction it is a journey and that they are the ones who are in charge of creating the features of that road.

If they need to build a bridge over a river in their journey, they can make that bridge look anyway they want. If they want the bridge to be precarious because they need something to support the tension of an escape, it can be a hanging bridge, with the ropes holding the bridge nearly severed. If they need a bridge full of confidence showing the characters going off into happy future, the bridge can be a suspension bridge like the Golden Gate or the Verrazano-Narrows bridge in New York's harbor, bridges that seemingly stretch forever with strength and eternal durability (unless of course they'd like to make a statement about questioning the idea of "happily ever after," in which case the treacherous hanging bridge would work very well!) The same is true for creating characters. Students create characters in fiction to serve certain purposes. They need to understand that all of their characters need not come "off-the-rack," but can be "custom made."

Helping Students Create Character Collages

- Some students may not even know what a collage is. So first then, simply experiment with creating collages out of various substances. You might want to show them pictures of the work of famous collagists in art books . . . Rauschenberg, Braque, Picasso, Ernst, et al. Talk with students about the process of collecting and combining images. Talk with them about how the process is similar to creating characters in their writings. Or have them teach you about collage by asking them to bring in some rap music (with "clean" lyrics). Rap music often is about collage or "sampling" bits and pieces from other music.

- Have students play with and make a book where the pages are divided into three sections and where they can put different "heads" together with a variety of "legs," a variety of "torsos," and so on. Also have them play with those magnet or cut-out games that have a variety of clothes and body parts. Have students continually create and name new characters as well as speculate on their character's personalities.
- Have students create a collage specifically of people. Have them first gather photos in magazines and pictures of people in comic strips and comic books and then create composite figures. Have them write about the personality of the person they've created, basing their texts on the different visual elements they've combined to create the whole.
- Next, have students create a fictional history and present for the "person" they've created.
- Choose a partner for each student at random. Have the students talk about how their collage characters met, what their relationship is to one another, and then have them create a dialogue having to do with the nature of their character's relationship.

DON'T FORGET THE SURPRISES

One final word about character that probably applies to writing in general. Help students to enjoy creating surprises and incongruities. Writing is most interesting to read when you are given unexpected twists and turns. For me, it is very satisfying when a "good" character reveals a "bad" side, or when someone who is perpetually fearful rises to the occasion and becomes heroic, or when someone who is funny unexpectedly reveals a serious side.

How can we encourage our students to be mentally flexible and to have the willingness and courage to experiment and to break from form?

- Take a story everyone knows, for example, *Three Little Pigs* or *Little Red Riding Hood*, and have students pick one character who suddenly acts in a different way than the story traditionally dictates. Have them write about how the unexpected behavior changes the nature of the story. Do the same for a cartoon, a comic book, a situation comedy character, or even with a newspaper story.
- Have students tell or write a story about something that actually happened to them, and have them change a way they acted in a certain situation and then consider the implications of that new action on the other characters and for the rest of the story.

- Have students take a traditional story and tell it from the perspective of another character. For instance, tell *Little Red Riding Hood* from the point of view of the wolf or *Cinderella* from the point of view of a "step sister."
- Have students make something unexpected happen to a character in a traditional, contemporary, or mass media-generated story. For instance, what would happen if Mickey Mouse suddenly grew to the size of a mountain? Would he be "cute" any longer? How would he react? Or how would the Tin Man, et al., react if Dorothy suddenly became inflicted with a "disease" that made her mean and insulting? Can students imagine Dorothy mean and moody? Would she try to fight this behavior or would she enjoy it?

I'm a little tired of writing. Maybe I can just stop writing and we can meet at a coffeehouse and talk about these ideas. That would be a surprise, wouldn't it? If you are sitting in your favorite café and in I walked? "Any questions about what you've read so far?" Why not? After all, coffeehouses have always been good places for conversations. Where do you like to meet your friends and talk? Certain places are better than others, for sure. That takes us to the next chapter . . . the role of *Place*.

Any suggestions about where to meet?

5

Finding and Using Place

Discussing the Role of Place in Writing

The trees under which we seek shade, the rivers and bays we cross by car, traverse by kayak, or roll by on bicycles; the old advertising signs disappearing on the sides of buildings; the graffiti lit by "work" lights inside of an otherwise darkened subway tunnel; the malls where we shop or socialize; the great grey expanse of a parking lot where we leave our cars; the manicured lawns of a suburban housing development; the bodegas where we purchase milk; the fields of corn that we will soon harvest . . . these are all part of our environmental context. This is where we live, work, dream, and play. It is what we are surrounded by, embraced by, frightened by, confused by, enchanted by, and disgusted with. This is what we want our students to pay attention to and to identify.

The darkening sky on a late New England autumn afternoon; the clear, crisp winter's visibility from a New Mexican mountain; the summer's lusciously wet southern bayou; the first warm spring day in New York City, Seattle, Chicago, or Boston . . . this is our environmental context as well . . . where we live and where our students live and the worlds their literary characters will inhabit.

The smells of the crisp early morning September air after a hot, humid August; the feeling of snow and wind against our faces during a blizzard;

the first smells of the beach after a long drive; the sound of small peeper frogs signaling the end of winter, all impact the way we feel. As do less "natural" experiences, like the summer's garbage on a city sidewalk; walking beside a forest of glass skyscrapers; inside a cement-filled urban plaza in the heat of a southwestern summer; strolling under a canopy of trees in a neighborhood of porch-fronted wooden bungalows built in the 1920s. We are in constant dialogue with our environment, built and "natural," trees and houses, weather and elevators.

> As much as we in our fast-paced world often ignore it, we are still very much a part of and affected by where we live, what we see, and how we feel. Our life stories take place within the context of our built and "natural" worlds.

How can we sensitize students to the way their environment affects them while helping them build a vocabulary that lets them describe what they experience?

This chapter is the *location* for learning about location/place, describing it, and looking at how it influences the behavior of your characters and the expectations and experiences of your audience.

First, let's ask why this is even important. Two reasons . . .

1. To add to our students' "bank" of potential metaphors and similes that will help them describe their own and their character's psychological worlds.

   For example . . . "I felt as confused as the swamp in a summer bayou." "My future felt as endless as the New Mexican sky in the winter." "After months of sadness I felt the first glimpse of possibility, like a city emerging from a prolonged winter." "A sense of foreboding came over me like the cold, late autumn clouds blanketing a northern New England sky."

2. To understand how situating stories inside of a specific environment helps give a story more of its intended effect.

   For example . . . After the film, I said good-bye to my friend and went out into the parking lot to get my car. At first I forgot where I had left it but finally, with the lot dark and nearly empty like the night sky above it, I saw my car way in the back end of the parking lot. The walk to it seemed endless, as if I was walking through a desert of concrete, with no sound and just the faint hint of a cold wind making me slightly uncomfortable . . . and then . . . I noticed . . . a car speeding toward me, with its bright lights heading like an arrow toward its target.

ONLY

DEVELOPING SENSITIVITY TO PLACE

- Have students name and describe a place where they felt happy, sad, scared, small, bored, important, confused, comfortable, and full of energy. These places could be where the students have visited or lived. Have students describe why they think they felt a particular way in a particular location. Ask them to identify why they might have felt the way they did.
- Ask students to describe the way weather affects them. How do they feel when it rains, snows, it's sunny, or muggy, etc? Have this discussion every day in your morning circle.
- Ask students to write down what settings in books or movies were the most memorable? Ask them how they think that setting added to the quality of the story or movie?
- Ask students: If different types of weather were people, describe what those people would be like. For instance, what icons are associated with certain seasons and why? Why is there someone called "Old Man Winter"?
- Have students visit as many of the following as they can, and ask them to describe how it looked and how they felt being there . . . a mall parking lot in the summer; a forest in the winter; a traffic jam; a beach on a hot summer day; a lake in the fall; a baseball stadium; a church, mosque, temple, or synagogue; a farm; a local food store or bodega; an urban back or front yard; a fast food restaurant; the local park; a public swimming pool; a parking garage; a Laundromat.
- Look at various landscape paintings and have students imagine what it feels like to be in the places depicted. Do the same with paintings that depict urban and suburban landscapes.
- Listen to Vivaldi's *Four Seasons*; find some Indian ragas that are connected to times of the day; listen to The Loving Spoonful's "Hot Town, Summer in the City," to Otis Redding's "Sitting on the Dock By the Bay," Bedrich Smetana's "The Moldau," and to other songs or compositions that refer to a season or place. Have students describe what it feels like to be inside the world depicted in the music. Ask them if they've felt similar feelings for comparable places and times.
- Have students choose one place to go to at different times of the day and year. Ask them to describe how the times of the day and the times of the year make the space look and feel differently.
- Ask students to go to a place that is crowded and one that is empty; and one that is small and one that is large. Have them describe how different each space felt.
- Ask students to go a park, play on something that is for younger kids, and then describe how it felt.

How can we help students use their insights into *place* in their writing?

1. Have students think about the books they've read and TV and movies they've watched. What kinds of stories have been situated in what kinds of environments . . . horror stories, comedies, mysteries, love stories, and dramas, for instance?

2. Have students write a paragraph or two about how a character feels walking through any environment they'd like. Have interested students draw a picture of this first.

3. Have students continue the above story but have something in the character's environment change. For instance, have it suddenly get cloudy or cold. Or have the character walk from a park into an elevator in an office building, or from a street near one's house into an unfamiliar neighborhood. How do these changes affect how the character feels and acts?

4. To mix things up a bit, have students create a character and have things happen to that character in environments that are not traditionally associated with the certain situations they are describing. For instance, have something funny happen to somebody in an environment that is considered traditionally "scary." Have a character have a "serious" discussion in a "fun house." Have a character be extremely joyous in a rain or snowstorm. Have a character experience romance in a decidedly unromantic setting, like the principal's office.

USING PLACE AS STORY STARTERS

Finding interesting situations in which to place people is always a good way to start a story. For example, what happens when five people get stuck in an elevator? Imagine a situation where a blizzard strands people together at a highway rest stop. Who can forget how the Humphrey Bogart movie *Key Largo* is set with the hurricane isolating a group of people with their tormentors . . . or how about Marilyn Monroe and her "friends" in the movie *Bus Stop*?

> Interesting places can lead to interesting scenarios where characters are forced to interact in interesting ways.

To help students find ways to begin stories using *place*, they must first become sensitive about physical location and its potential for creating opportunities for interesting situations to unfold.

RECOGNIZING HOW PLACE AFFECTS BEHAVIOR

First, students need to pay attention to how space creates *behavior expectancy*. How do people normally behave in elevators, in places of worship, in places where they are waiting for a bus, train, or plane? How do people interact in a department store, a convenience store, a movie theater ticket line, or a locker room? You might have students write about places they've been or have visited in a span of, say, two weeks and write about *situational behavior*. Have them make a list of interesting places where relatively small numbers of people gather (not, for instance, a baseball stadium). The list might include elevators, stores of various kinds, basements, locker rooms, a tent in the woods, and an airline terminal. Ask students to list various things that could happen either inside or outside this space that would affect how people would interact and behave differently than usual. For instance, the power is shut off and there is a tornado outside; the roof leaks during a hurricane; or the heat in a building won't shut off and (for some reason) the windows can't be opened and no one can leave.

Ask students to dramatize these scenarios. Let them play with these situations for a while. When you feel they have continued long enough, shout out a new variable. For instance, pretend that people are caught inside an office with no exit and the heat won't turn off; then you suddenly announce that the air conditioner comes on and it gets colder and colder.

Another exercise that can be done theatrically is to have students choose from a list of environments, determine the characters in that environment, create a "situation" for those characters, and then "let it roll."

Remember, sometimes the body has to move before the brain can.

CREATING AN IMAGINARY LANDSCAPE

In a world where books, movies, and video games encourage an appreciation of "magical" landscapes, your students will gravitate toward this kind of writing. I don't encourage this at first because using "outer space" and fictitious environments often becomes a crutch for students, not unlike the "deus ex machina" of 19th century literature where an angel comes down to earth, ends a story, and resolves a problem that an author obviously had difficulty solving. With that said, it is interesting to explore the basic physical elements of our universe to prepare the way for future explorations of the imagined worlds. Consider the following:

Gravity

What would it be like if it seemed that people could walk without gravity affecting them?

Temperature

How would people adapt to a landscape of heat or cold way more extreme than anything humans have experienced. How could it affect how they look and behave?

Moisture

How would people adapt to living under water all the time?

Soft or Bouncy

How would people move in such an environment?

I'm sure that your students could come up with many more improvisations on *environment*. Let them do that for a while. It will help them to do two things . . .

- Make them more aware of the physical constraints of our environment.
- Understand how an environment can shape much of who we are.

You can also enlist science teachers by asking them to help students look at how their environment affects their body and behavior and to help them speculate how it would be changed from a "changed" environment. It is also true that many people around the world continue to experience nature as full of magic . . . stones that contain visions, trees that speak, mountains that are considered holy. Again, reading science fiction and looking at myth and folklore can help young people be aware that not everyone interprets and therefore interacts with the world in the way that they do. If students want to create writing that challenges our own "truths" about the physical laws that govern so much of our beliefs, behavior, and physical appearance, they must do so only after having a good understanding of those "laws" as well as about other beliefs and "truths" that motivated the behavior of those who followed an alternative understanding of the world.

Speaking of motivation . . . it's a problem with students sometimes, isn't it?

6

Motivating Students

Writing Across Disciplines, Genres, Classroom Boundaries, and Into the World!

In this chapter, we will look at how to help students embrace and be excited about writing, how to help them get through the inevitable frustrations inherent in the learning process, and how to help them learn to write in various genres utilizing what they already know.

A quick personal story . . . In eleventh grade I was sort of a "cub" sports reporter for our high school newspaper, the *Forest Hills Beacon,* assigned to cover not the "big" sports like basketball or baseball but to cover the comparatively "minor" events like track meets, where I also happened to be a participant. Now I was never a very motivated student. I wasn't a bad student, just not a very good one. My elementary school principal always said to me as he gave me my report card, "You can do better!" Some things came pretty easily to me and some didn't and, while I pretended to study at night at my desk, most of my homework was done in spurts of very short duration or to the accompaniment and ultimately distraction of a baseball or basketball game on the radio. However, when I had an article to write about a track event, I was obsessed . . . obsessed with finding the correct metaphors, the right flow, and the most engaging leads. With leads for instance, I just loved the process of looking for the right sentence or two that would distill the essence of my story, while whetting the reader's appetite for finding out more.

I remember one particular night when I was awake past 11:00 p.m., nearing midnight, going over and over various combinations of words for my lead. My mother came out into the living room. After I read a few of my openings to her she said, with some disappointment, that she wished I could have devoted as much time to my schoolwork, as I did to finding a lead for my story. At that time, nearing the age of 16, I luckily realized that I didn't have to feel guilty about my comparative lack of attention to math, social studies, and French. I realized that I was working so hard at my sports writing because I valued what I was doing, had confidence it my ability to get it "right," and knew that others would see and appreciate my work.

> Most of us seem to learn best when we understand why we are learning something and what purpose it will eventually serve.

There were some of us who did well in school because we wanted to be "good" like our teacher; we understood that successfully completing the assignment was one step on a ladder we wanted to climb; or we just enjoyed the style of teaching employed at the time. Unfortunately for most of us, repetitive and contrived work was a chore and something we rushed through, more often than not, without any thought. While again it might be strictly anecdotal, it seems now more and more difficult to get kids to do work simply because they are told to do it. Could it be that students feel the pressure to succeed at tests coming from teachers and administrators and feel the lack of joy and purpose conveyed in the process of teaching?

For us to succeed as teachers we need to find *real life, beyond teachers' eyes*, and *authentic* reasons for students to write, and we need to help students feel that the effort they spend perfecting their craft will have personal and social payoff; not unlike skateboarders practicing their jumps, basketball players their moves, or dancers their leaps and turns.

LEARNING HOW TO LEARN

I've never been a good learner. I admit it and perhaps because of that, I might have an insight into what is needed to help students become "good learners." What does it mean to be a good learner? Well, having patience, confidence, and diligence. My problem with learning was that I was either frustrated by my initial "incompetence" or, if I initially and superficially succeeded, I wasn't motivated to push myself further. (It could also be that I was lazy, but here is not the place to entertain those thoughts.)

Learning anything is a complex dance of expectation, frustration, and exaltation. For students to take the stages of learning in stride and not become either overconfident from momentary successes or disengaged by temporary failure, we need to engage them first in a discussion of learning.

How? Here are some ideas. Early in the school year, ask students to list the skills they have consciously learned in their lives. Have they learned how to ride a bicycle, play the piano, jump rope, or do a cartwheel? Once you've had that discussion, have students discuss and identify the different stages in their learning process. First, ask them to tell you why they wanted to learn a particular skill? How did they decide to learn it? Did they watch others or have a teacher? Were they scared when they started to learn? Were they worried about how others would react to their mistakes and failures? Did they ever feel frustrated? Did they ever want to give up? How did they overcome those feelings? Did they enjoy the process all the time? What were the hardest stages in their learning? What made them want to continue? How did they practice? Did they have a schedule? Did they recognize the fact there were different stages in the learning process and that they would reach certain "plateaus" and then fall back down for a while? Do they remember any funny things that happened when they were learning?

Building Skills

- It's important for students to understand that mastering certain skills in their lives is not always easy. Students need to recognize that they have a reservoir of resiliency when it comes to learning; resiliency that has helped them in the past to get through seemingly insurmountable difficulties. It would also help if you could share some of the trials and tribulations of your learning as well. How about sharing your "first day as a teacher" story?

- Ask students to read books about athletes, musicians, news anchors, writers, dancers, glassblowers, scholars, teachers, and others who discuss how they practiced and perfected their craft. Have students interview their parents, older siblings and other relatives and neighbors as well. Discuss these books and interviews during morning circle. Make a list of the different stages in the learning process and of the tactics used by the famous and not so famous to overcoming frustration and to "keep going." Call it the *Keep Going List*!
- Have students pick one thing to learn during the school year, outside of the necessities of school. It can be anything that requires some effort and that is interesting to them. Have students keep a *learning journal* in which they record their progress each day. Give each student a chart that includes all the different phases of learning that have already been discussed (initial reluctance, frustration with first stages, and so on), and each day have students check off which part of the learning process they experienced. Now here's the hard part . . . teachers should learn something as well! Come on, you know there are things that you want to learn; things that you tell your friends like, "I've always wanted to learn how to kayak, knit, play guitar, etc." There should be time set aside in morning circle to discuss how *everyone* is doing with their "learning."
- If you have the facility to do this, have each student (and yourself) grow a plant from seed. Check on and nurture the plant each day. The plant can be a visual metaphor for learning in that it requires attention and patience and is often frustrating. Sure, some of the seeds will be unable to grow and or will just die, but encourage students to figure out why and seek either to rectify the problem, or, if it is too late, plant another seed. By planting and watching a seed grow, you will have something to refer to (along with the other exercises) when students become frustrated with the pace of their learning. Besides, kids love to grow things. You can also have students maintain a diary of their efforts and of the plant's growth each day.
- Have students be "learning coaches" for each other, inspiring their partners to continue when they get frustrated.
- Find stories to tell students about folklore and real-life people who succeeded at accomplishing something, in spite of difficulties. I love the story that my friend Len Cabral tells about the mouse that falls into a pitcher of cream and is unable to get out. Nearly giving up, the mouse decides instead to push forward and moves its legs so quickly that it turns the cream into whipped cream, allowing it to climb out from its liquid trap.

WRITING FOR A PURPOSE

Many adults write every day either for personal or professional reasons. Let's make a list of some of the professions where writing is a big part of what people do.

- Authors of novels and non-fiction work
- Magazine writers
- Newspaper reporters
- Writers for a TV series and the evening news
- Cartoonists
- Script writers for the movies
- Play, movie, and book critics
- Technical writers who give you directions on how to operate machines
- Policy people who work for legislators
- Advertising copywriters
- Publicity agents
- Lawyers writing briefs
- Scientists documenting results of studies
- Gossip and advice columnists
- Bloggers

Obviously many people write for a living and communicate with the written word. There are many ways to make your writing public, as you no doubt realize. Most of the time, "making your work public" in school involves seeing your writing posted in the hall in a "best writing" area or reading your work at a publishing party attended by another class and a reluctant principal or vice-principal who most likely prefers to be dealing with mountains of paperwork instead. We still tend to isolate our wonderfully expansive and potentially engaged young people behind the walls of a schoolroom, giving them little opportunity to participate in the world through the power of their ideals, ideas, concerns, and the force of their writing. When we ask students to write, we too often give them prompts that are mostly contrived and as meaningless as the old, "What did you do during your summer vacation?"

Actually, let's look at that cliché to see if it can actually be used to engage students in the "real" world. As we do this, I realize that this prompt is a cliché and that many prompts have a much higher level of specificity and interest. However, because it is such a stereotype, I think it will be helpful in our attempts at making writing more meaningful.

OK, here we go . . . being interested in finding out about how your students spent their summer is certainly important. No question. But when we ask students to write about what they did during the summer, does that mean we are really showing that we care about how they spent that potentially significant time of the year? Ask yourself, why would students care to write about it? How many teachers who have given that assignment first engage their students in a dialogue about their own and their student's July and August? How many teachers who have given that assignment first have their students talk to each other about what the summer meant to them? How many teachers who have used this prompt asked themselves why they wanted their students to spend valuable time on this particular question?

These are hard questions to answer and to face because many of us are doing to our students what we have had done to us . . . because it "worked for us, didn't it?" But remember, most of the time, it really didn't work. Most of us (face it now) really don't like to write and feel that we can't write and have nothing to say anyway. Most of us think writing is a chore. It is the same for most students. A prompt without a context, without purpose, without an interesting end in sight, *is* a chore!

Now, let's take the prompt, "What did you do during the summer?" and see if we can make it interesting and engaging. Like I said, asking students how they spent their last two months free from the constraints of school is certainly a valid question, especially as they walk into your classroom for the first time in the fall. Their answers would certainly help you to get to know them a little bit, assure them that you are interested in who they are, let them know a little about each other, and help them to think reflectively and descriptively.

First, though, if you are genuinely interested in what your students did during the summer, have a discussion in morning circle. Let everyone have a chance to give a general description of their life without school. Allow students to ask each other questions about their experiences. You can ask questions as well (and certainly tell what you did during the summer too). Raise some interesting issues . . . Do you like being in school or out of school better? Why? What would your ideal summer have been like? What was one thing you learned during the summer (not necessarily a skill, but perhaps something about life)? Did you go on any trips, visit any relatives? Were you bored? How did it feel to be bored? In other words the question, "What did you do during the summer?", needs clarification. It is just too large. You might as well say, "Write about your life."

Next, what are you going to do with the answers? Can this information be used as part of a larger writing project? Can you find a way for your students' stories to have an audience beyond your tired eyes? Of course you can. You can encourage them to bring in pictures of their summer vacations. You can put the stories of their summer vacations on a bulletin board outside the classroom. You can stimulate a discussion around the school about the issues you've talked and written about by sending out surveys to other classes. Have the results tabulated (math?) and organized and presented attractively in a public spot in your school so that parents coming in can see the results and contribute information about how *they* spent their summers when they were kids. Ask students to conduct oral histories with their parents as another way to gather this information. Have them find out whether their parents have pictures of vacations or camps they attended. You can set up a Web site with a blog or a Wiki to encourage students elsewhere to share their experiences. Also look at how summer vacations have changed over the years and how people spend summer vacations in other parts of the world.

From the results of these surveys and oral histories, can we generate interest in studying about old nearby amusement parks, summer camps, and family vacations? How about contemporary amusement parks . . . how were they constructed (science?), publicized, etc.? Can we trace summer drives that students and their parents took when they were younger (geography)? For older students, can we look at *summer romance* as a topic to investigate through oral history, literature, song, and memoir? Can part of your *summer vacation project* involve looking at letters, text messages, and e-mails written between parent and child or between friends and even studying the different forms of communication that existed for different generations? Can you look at the topic of *missing* . . . that is, missing people, when you or they are away? Or looking at the difference between *country* and *city* for those of us lucky enough to get away from an urban environment? Many kids see relatives and go to family reunions . . . pictures and descriptions of those would certainly be interesting as part of our exhibit.

Let's face it: Many kids don't get a chance to do much in the summer. Parents are working, money isn't available; so kids are often left to fend for themselves, which can mean anything from impromptu games in the streets, eyes locked to TV and video games, or city or social agency-sponsored recreation camps. What are these experiences like? Can students and parents rally city agencies for better summer programming by writing persuasive letters (genre studies!) to city hall or other government agencies? Can students write histories of summer camps or summer recreation centers?

I'm getting tired from all this work! You know, I was skeptical at first, but now I think it might be a good idea . . . if it is meaningful. What is a meaningful project?

> A project is meaningful if its intent is clear, if it can have an audience beyond the eyes of the teacher, if there are models in the particular form of writing that you're working on, if the topic can arise out of a discussion that includes your students, and if the topic or presentation can lead to other new and exciting areas of study.

Let's take a variety of genre and modes of presentation that would be meaningful for your students.

Memoirs

- Find a topic that students have in common with one another: getting lost; first boy/girl party; sibling rivalries; food preferences; stubbornness; dealing with bullies; excuse making; wanting to wear clothes, hair, and jewelry not accepted by parents; grown-up activities they must attend, like parties or religious observances, and have students talk and then write about this subject. Find other authors who have dealt with similar topics and read their books to students. Decide what you want to do with these memoirs. Will they be put into a book, organized around a particular topic, and accompanied by relevant photos and drawings? Will the topics be explored with other classes through surveys? Will the topics be explored with parents? Why don't you create a literary magazine that collects and presents all of this material?
- Have each student create a map of their neighborhood and have them mark important *memoir* points on their map. These places should be locations where things important to your students have happened . . . learning how to ride bikes, meeting friends, scraping knees, getting lost. Have students accompany the "maps with memoirs" that describe these events. Put the maps and the stories in a public spot in your school. Go out into the community and encourage storeowners and neighbors to create their own *neighborhood memoir maps*. Maybe your "neighbors" will give you their maps and stories for you to display or perhaps they will permit some of you to show your work in their store windows. Create a Web site that includes these stories and becomes visible when the cursor moves over the place where these events occurred.
- Create a shoe day, a stuffed animal day, a "collection" day, etc., and have students bring in an item relevant to the day's theme and a story of why the particular object is important to them or a family member. Present both the objects and stories in a central part of your school and encourage other classes to participate. Study and write about the history of shoes and cobblers. (Did you know that as far back as the Roman Empire and into the Middle Ages cobblers were considered the intellectuals of the craftsmen? Then, as now, people would gather in their shops and discuss important political and cultural events. Their symbol was the crow, an animal that had the power to go into the world of the "dark" and of the "night").

Reporting

- Create a school newspaper, TV show, or radio show (using your school's PA system) and divide up and rotate reporting tasks that can include school news, sports (including less traditional sports like skateboarding and surfing), movies, video games and book

reviews, editorials, neighborhood history, and things to do in the neighborhood. Bring in local reporters and editors, bloggers, etc., to discuss their respective crafts.

- See if your class can establish a relationship with a local TV, radio station, or newspaper and agree to contribute a segment or column on various topics of concern to children. When I was about 12, I wrote to all of the then nine local newspapers to get a job as a reviewer of children's movies . . . unfortunately, I was turned down. Hopefully you won't be.
- Establish a blog or a Web site where students could comment on issues of concern to young people. Find a way to publicize these sites and to be in dialogue with students in other parts of the city, state, nation, and world.

PERSUASIVE WRITING

To learn persuasive writing, students need to care about something, feel they are addressing the appropriate person, and believe they can make a difference and be a catalyst for change. Do most students have a history of persuading others that can be used as your *foundational knowledge*? You bet they do!

To begin, discuss with students times when they tried to persuade someone to do or allow something. For instance, I'm sure your students at one time or another tried to get their parents to allow them to stay up past bedtime. Or maybe they wanted to go somewhere, wear a certain type of clothing, or adopt a certain hairstyle. Have students write a persuasive letter to the appropriate person about one of these everyday topics. What would the components of such a letter be?

Initiating a general discussion of this would work. Should they yell at someone? Should they make the person feel disrespected? Should they say they will "get back" at the person if they don't do as they are trying to get them to do?

Ask students to try to persuade you to, say, forget about homework for a week. Would they just say, "Pretty, pretty, please, no homework?" They might try, but depending on your mood and patience, it probably would not work. Let them know that you have your reasons for giving homework, and it isn't just to be "mean."

> When writing a persuasive letter, students must understand that they need to appeal and address the specific interests and concerns of the person to whom they are writing.

For instance, you probably give homework to help students practice what they are learning in school. If students are going to be successful in convincing you not to give homework, they must first address why you felt it was important to give. Should they say that when they do the homework at home they can't concentrate on it and that it doesn't really help them? Should they say they are too tired at home to do homework? Should they say that homework creates fights with their parents? Should they say they feel their time would be better spent on "free reading" rather than on math? Should they say they understand the importance of working on something after school and wonder if they can just do it, say, one day rather than four days per week? I'm not sure how I would argue it but having a discussion about the importance of "knowing where someone is coming from," is a good idea, as is "trying on" different arguments against anticipated counterarguments.

Where does one find persuasive writing and discussion? Letters to the editor is one place; town hall meetings are another. If you can find age appropriate versions of these, have students go to important town hall meetings and look at editorials and letters to the editor to see if they can see what makes for good ones. Having people who write editorials for local newspapers speak to your class is another way to develop an understanding of what it takes to craft a good persuasive letter. Another idea is to bring someone in who receives a lot of persuasive letters—a council person or a town manager—and have them discuss what kind of letters make them think and take action.

Here are some basic elements of a persuasive letter.

- Introduce yourself politely and clearly
- Simply state what you desire

- Clarify why you are choosing to write that specific person
- Defend your position in a way that is understandable and acceptable to the recipient
- Quickly restate what you need or your intent
- End the letter pleasantly

Next, in our efforts to teach persuasive writing, have students seriously consider what changes they would want to make in the running of their school . . . more gym . . . less math . . . more drinking fountains? Have them write a persuasive letter to the principal advocating for those changes. Help students understand that form and tone are as important in letter writing as is the type of clothing required for attending a White House party.

DON'T FORGET "SITE SPECIFIC" FORMS OF COMMUNICATION

Many young people today conduct most of their "real-world" writing through text messaging, IM (instant messaging), blogging, and other Web-based sites. In the interest of time, money, usage, and related issues, these types of communications have developed their own rules for spelling, grammar, and punctuation. These include new abbreviations, new needs for brevity, and different priorities for "depth." There are new expectations for these new forms of communications, just as surely as the written letter had its own. To communicate differently through these mutually created and accepted conventions would not let you be part of this "world." Imagine receiving a Proustian paragraph as a text message? In the same way that young people learn they can communicate with their friends in one way and their grandparents and hopefully their parents in another, they need to realize that purpose and audience demand different forms of writing. Although, that said, it is probably only a matter of time when some of the conventions from text messaging become acceptable in other forms of communication. There are already novels created initially for the phone screens . . . and who will be the first U.S. president with a tattoo? The ways in which acceptable conventions mutate is interesting but maybe a little beside the point. Suffice it to say that . . .

> Form, grammar, spelling, and so on were not given on Mt. Sinai. They are culturally agreed upon conventions, necessary to navigate certain societal arenas. Students need to realize that tone and form are part of understanding how to successfully navigate the world around them. If they want to operate in certain arenas, they have to know what is expected of them.

GETTING BACK TO PERSUASION

Take a walk with your students around the neighborhood and look for various things that need improvement, like potholes, more stoplights, broken playgrounds, dangerously fast traffic, and too few shade trees. Brainstorm about whom they might write (a good social studies and civics lesson!) and then write a letter to the appropriate person or agency.

The next steps they might take, depending upon the response, include:

- Write a petition for other students or neighbors to sign.

  Writing a petition is a particular form of writing . . . short, succinct, to the point, strongly stated, without rancor, and yet with a sense of urgency. Again, find a petition and have your students dissect it.

- Write a letter or editorial for a local paper.

  With many models to work from, this is a good way to help students prepare and state an argument. Ask them, as always, to consider their audience and their purpose for writing. A good letter to a newspaper is clear, readable, interesting, and demonstrates a sincere concern for the topic at hand. A good editorial clearly states the problem being addressed up front and then makes a case for its solution, while acknowledging and reacting to other attempts to rectify the problem being considered.

- Write a letter to a TV or a radio station, asking them to do a story on a particular neighborhood problem.

  Here is where being a kid helps. A group of students crafting a letter asking for publicity for a particular campaign is almost a guarantee for success . . . and great TV! A letter requesting publicity should give the reporters a sense of how important a particular issue is to the community. It should also promise some visuals, especially if you are writing to a TV station (know your audience and their needs.). For instance, "There will be 20 third graders wearing yellow vests, trying to cross the street." Before writing your letter, it would be valuable to call up a media outlet and ask someone in charge of scheduling what kind of letter they tend to respond to . . . or even better, ask someone from a local TV station to come into your school. Tell students to remember that TV and radio stations are busy and that their available "on-air" time is limited. Not only do you often have to show them how your story stands out conceptually and visually, but also you must at times tell them how to position the story and how it could look or sound.

> Again, it is important that you find models for the above forms so that your students will have something to "shoot for." One of the advantages for having *real* reasons to write is that you can always find "real-world" models from which to learn.

As students get older, they can take on more abstract issues, such as war and peace, justice, and first amendment issues, and they can either write locally or nationally to newspapers, blogs, Wikis, etc. Developing student skills in interacting with the civic community is important for preserving our country's democratic traditions, while promoting deep thinking and confidence in one's ideas and ability to express them.

Other Forms of "Real-World" Writing

- Create a literary magazine in your school, grade, or class.
- Have a regularly scheduled after school or evening "coffeehouse" during which students, teachers, and parents bring writing to share.
- Work with the local chamber of commerce, realtor association, or economic development office to create a brochure or a Web site extolling the virtues of your neighborhood for kids. Describe the parks, restaurants, food stores, and shops that young people would be interested in knowing about as their parents consider living there.
- Create a museum in your school. The exhibits could highlight local history; oral histories of parents, staff, and neighbors; favorite student collections; historical or cultural exploration; etc. Having a museum gives you a lot of opportunities to explore various types of writing including text for the exhibit, labels, invitations to openings, and catalogues.
- Develop and publicize a blog to discuss issues of concern for students.
- Create a product to sell and market.

PRACTICING THE CRAFT OF REVISING AND EDITING

> The more students understand why they are writing and the more they have models to which to aspire, the more the task of polishing and editing becomes easier to encourage.

When students understand that their work is going to be seen by an entire school community, or by a newspaper editor or mayor, the more they will feel a sense of urgency about working on their piece to ensure that it will have its intended effect and won't embarrass them. Certainly, it will continue to be necessary for you to "look over their shoulders" and to have their "writing buddies" do the same, but the more students have a say about what they write and have embraced *why* they are writing, the more polishing and perfecting becomes an internal or intrinsic versus an external or extrinsic mandate. During this revising and editing phase, it is important to go back to the part of this chapter where we talk about learning *how* to learn and keep emphasizing that *no craft worth perfecting comes without effort*!

Revising

Revising is making sure the intent of your writing and the final product are aligned, and that your narrative proceeds sequentially, without gaps or unexplained and extraneous tangents.

Students hate revising, don't they? I don't really like it myself, although there is a beauty to organizing, simplifying, and distilling. It is kind of like spring cleaning, organizing your files, or giving away clothes to make room in your closet. You dread doing it, but you are ultimately happier because of your efforts. To encourage students to appreciate revising, start with some activities that will give them a visceral understanding of what they are about to do.

- Ask your students to clean a desk, a closet, a garage and toss away things they feel they no longer need. Have them describe in writing, the process, from beginning to end, their purpose, their resistance, their choices, and ultimately how they feel, once it is done.
- Have students describe an event such as a sporting match, a party, or a drive. Have them write their descriptions in increasingly smaller and smaller increments. Depending on the age of your students, have them start with, say, a two-page description, then a one-page description, then a half-page, and then a paragraph. The goal is to have them remove more and more nonessential description until the description is distilled to its essence.
- Give each student a piece of soap. Have them carve something of their own choice. Ask them to tell you what they are carving. This of course is similar to the revising process, knowing your intent and making sure the results match.

Revising, however, not only means subtracting the extraneous but also looking for gaps in the narrative. Hopefully, some of the work you've done previously with your students using sequential thinking will help them to find their errors, either as they go through the work themselves or with the aid of their writing buddy. Try to encourage students to read their work out loud to themselves and their writing partner. Adding this additional step often helps students to find errors easier than just by reading.

Editing

Editing is noticing the details. Spelling, punctuation, run-on sentences, poor word choice . . . the things that make one's manuscript look and read amateurish or professional, polished or sloppy, kared (whoops . . . cared) for or rushed through.

Editing is also a meditative practice. What do I mean by this? Am I going really off the deep end now? Editing requires concentration. It asks us to see the particulars that make up the whole. When we teach our children to edit, we are also teaching them to concentrate and to focus, certainly skills they'll need as they get older.

Let's look at some ways to encourage concentration.

- Any kind of meditative practice is valuable. Simply sitting still and noticing your breath come in and out of your body is a good start.
- The card game of "concentration" is a fun way to build these muscles. Do you know the game? You take the 52 cards, lay them out face down, choose one and then another with the goal of trying to match the number previously taken. If there is no match, you have to put the cards back where you found them, leaving the next person the task of finding a match, now armed with the knowledge of those cards' location.
- Find some of those pictures where there are objects added that are inappropriate to the setting, either because of time or place. Like for instance, a picture of a 17th century colonial village with a big Buick in the center or, maybe, a tropical rainforest with a snowman. If you can't find them, create them yourself. Once the students get a sense of what you're doing, let them create them for each other.

The key, though, to encourage students to edit or polish is to have a genuine reason for doing so, an audience and a purpose that demands attention to detail.

WRITING ACROSS THE CURRICULUM

There is nothing exotic about what has now fashionably been called *writing across the curriculum*. Again, it is just finding authentic reasons to write in whatever activity students are immersed. Most professions utilize a certain amount of writing skills. It can be as simple as writing suggestions to a boss or as complicated as creating a plan to reorganize a school district. For students, writing across the curriculum means utilizing their writing skills to reflect, to comment upon, to find and make connections, and to share knowledge from the various subject areas being studied.

Here are some examples of including writing for a purpose within various curriculum disciplines:

Social Studies

Let's say your class is studying how the neighborhood works: learning about the fire department, the post office, the sanitation workers, the police, etc. First, if possible, leave the classroom and actually walk out into the community so that you can see these people at work. Find a way to interview these government employees, take their photographs doing various activities, get tours of their facilities, and then combine all of these in either a book or a display for others to see.

Let's quickly brainstorm some of the questions that students might ask, say, a sanitation worker:

- What do you do?
- What do you like best and least in your job?
- Have you ever picked up something really funny? What?
- What is the most interesting experience you've had on the job?
- Are there seasonal differences in your work? Can you describe them?
- What time do you get to work and what time do you leave?
- What is your favorite time of the day? Why?
- Are there differences in the types of things you see in different neighborhoods? Like what?
- How did you learn your work?
- How did you get your job?

If you see someone doing a particularly exemplary job, write a complimentary letter to that person's boss or to the newspaper. Write stories imagining oneself in a particular job. Write letters to other countries to ask about civil servants abroad and write back about yours locally.

Maybe your class is learning about world geography. Start by examining the national backgrounds of your students. Have students research and write about *their* heritage, incorporating some oral histories with family members. They also could find out about contemporary life in those countries by writing letters to international schools and/or American embassy sites. (The embassy or international school could introduce them to schools in the community that are proficient in English.) Students could survey people in the neighborhood to learn their backgrounds. They could write up the results of the survey and send it to a local newspaper. Some of the survey questions could be:

- What do you consider your national background? Why?
- What do you know about that country?
- What other countries form parts of your heritage?
- What family rituals or traditions observed by your family were celebrations and rituals in your previous country?

Depending upon the age of your students you can ask them to write about what national origin means to them. Or have them notice examples of how what "being American" changes as the result of immigration. How do foods, language, and stores reflect a country in constant transition? Again, depending on the age of your students, help them to notice and write about examples of cultural fusion . . . in themselves or in the culture in general, for example, Kimchi pizza, Thai bagel shop, Spanglais, and Reggaton.

When studying history, ask students to create memoirs from the point of view of participants in battles, strikes, politics, family relations, work, etc., to get them imagining and thinking within a particular time and place. Share these stories in some way, perhaps theatrically or through CDs created and available for your school or community. Have students write editorials for old newspapers taking sides in the political conflicts of different eras. Have the older students write short pieces of historical fiction taking place in the times and places that you are studying.

Science

Science really lends itself to writing. Following the progress of a seed, as we discussed in an earlier chapter, is just one example. The scientific method involves speculation and observation or hypothesis and testing, all of which of course involves writing.

TAKING A DETOUR WITH A QUICK STORY . . .

There was a very fine teacher I worked with in Providence, Rhode Island, who really wanted to do an inquiry-based project but was unable to figure one out. She had some small frogs she brought into the class. They all unfortunately died after two days. She brought more in. They died as well. Her children asked, why? They speculated or created different hypothesis and called in "experts." They came up with the theory that there was a problem in using tap water for the aquarium. The year ended and they didn't have time to test this theory . . . perhaps lucky for any new little frogs. The teacher, a very good one, said that she still wasn't sure how to do an inquiry project. "Excuse me," I said, "What do you think you were doing?"

Had this teacher embraced the "mystery of the dead frogs" as an inquiry project, imagine the writing that could have come out of it. The class could have been divided into teams of researchers, with each group responsible for studying about a different variable in the care of the frogs: water, temperature, numbers, and food, and their reports and observations could have been written down and shared with the entire class. At the end of the research and after the mystery had been hopefully unraveled, the students could have compiled a final report, based on their initial speculation, research, and observations.

Articulating interests and curiosity, posing theories, researching and sharing observations, testing hypothesis, and compiling results are all opportunities for writing. You can see how long it takes a block of ice to melt at various temperatures, guess when the final leaf will be off the tree outside your school in the fall, build a structure that floats utilizing only toothpicks, build a bridge with paper that can withstand an agreed upon amount of weight, see best what substances can conduct heat . . . it doesn't matter. Writing can and should be part of any scientific investigation. It lets students reflect on what is being observed and helps them to articulate their conclusions. A classroom science journal is a good idea. In the more speculative realm, having students read and write science fiction is always a good way to encourage one's imagination and to integrate science and literacy.

If the science experiments are meaningful; if there is a reason you are doing the study (like with the frogs or seeds or, say, trying to figure out why a pipe in the basement leaks at certain times and not others), so much the better. As with any subject, meaningful work is better than work that is contrived, but nonetheless science and writing are *always* authentic partners!

USING ART AS A SPRINGBOARD TO WRITING

Many great artists of all disciplines were great writers, and certainly most were great readers. Art and writing have often been important to one another. Whether the artists are writing to develop their theories, to keep a diary to record impressions and observations, or writing letters to other artists to discuss the trials, tribulations, and celebrations of the artist's work, writing has served the artist in many ways.

Writing can also serve many functions for students who are studying as well as making art. At the end of each class, allow students some time to reflect on what was learned. At home, students can write about their progress in their chosen art form. They can write about their newly emerging aesthetic and the cultural and social events that are contributing to their growing "sophistication" (for example, concerts, museums, theater, movies, people watching). Students can write about working in different media and articulate their pleasures and difficulties in those arenas. They can also use writing to reflect upon how their skills are changing and evolving.

Older students can look at art history and write critiques of certain types of paintings, sculpture, and installations. They can debate abstraction versus representational art, and video art versus plastic arts; they can argue (in writing) about the merits or problems with graffiti; they can write editorials about the appropriateness of certain kinds of public art; and they can study about monuments built and planned and suggest monuments for the future. The history of art criticism is full of these kinds of debates. For example, the discussions about how sculpturally to memorialize 9/11 in New York City and the Holocaust in Berlin have led to many, many pages of writing.

A painting, a photograph, a video, or a sculpture can lead to written speculations about the artist's intent and about the way the work of art affects the viewer. Students can speculate about the personalities of those depicted in paintings, sculptures, and photographs; about the nature of social worlds depicted in anything from Parisian Boulevards to Gauguin's *Tahiti*, a George Segal sculpture, the qualities of the landscape in a Hudson River School painting, or a Georgia O'Keefe New Mexican desert evocation. In addition, students can write to galleries, museums, and the artists themselves to ask for information to better understand why a certain artist chooses to work with more difficult to comprehend styles . . . a black canvas, a strange video, or an odd installation, for instance. If you have galleries or museums with easy access, students can go and write reviews of the works they see.

Interestingly there are places in the visual arts where the worlds of letters and traditional and new media (video, installations, LED signs) completely converge. These include collage, where newspaper articles and advertisements (and even small bits of musical scores) find their way onto canvases, and the paintings of Jasper Johns and Robert Indiana, where letters and words are included as part of the painting. This is a great way to help students explore the nature of language, by having students make art that includes words and letters. Also look at the work of artist Jenny Holzer, who uses spiritual and political aphorisms in her appropriation of commercial and industrial signage. Your students can do this as well, by fashioning little bits of cultural truths into public art projects.

There is also art that memorializes events and places of historical or cultural importance. The works of Dolores Hayden and Lucy Lippard are important in this regard. In this kind of art, artists can combine sculptural forms that originate from the historic echoes of the site while utilizing language to further educate viewers. Student can work on these kinds of projects as well, incorporating history and text with site and art.

Writing across the curriculum is not magic. It is just good integrated teaching and learning!

LOOKING AT GENRE

In this section, I would like to look at how writing in various genres can be made easier to teach and to understand. When we teach different genres we often start with definitions and written texts rather than looking at what's available from the lives and experiences of our students. Ignoring the fortress-like armory that I mentioned at the beginning of the book is a good example of this. We were teaching fantasy writing yet ignoring what would have been a great springboard into thinking about fantasy.

> Too often we start with formula rather than from *real life*. Writing ultimately comes from experiences, whether it's real life or from a combination of real life and an author's imagination. Characters, situations, and settings are all drawn from sources that writers usually have experienced in whole or in part.

Let's take *horror* writing as an example. Kids (and adults for that matter) are scared of many things: houses that creek and groan in the night; wind that howls through windows; dogs in the neighborhood; "haunted" houses, closets, and the space under beds. We have all had experiences with something that scared us. Why not start discussions of horror writing with verbal accounts of stories about scared students? Let's look at these stories to see how tension built and then came to a head. Let's use these stories to demonstrate how fears grow, how the mind imagines, and how the story is resolved. Once we've demystified horror stories, we can show how other writers work within that genre. With horror writing and with other forms of writing, students must realize that they can be writers not just because they can imitate others but because they have their own experiences to share!

Let's look at other genres. How about *tall tales*; a great genre for kids? What student doesn't know how to exaggerate and to make things up? For instance, the fish they caught; the ball they hit; and the excuse they created for not bringing in their homework. *Tall tales* are also a good way to "tap in" to the way a young person looks at a world where everything is so much bigger, the weather is so much more intense, and everyone seems so much stronger and smarter than they are. Once this is accessed, it can be built on to create work in this genre.

Legends

I do one-person shows about Johnny Appleseed and Marco Polo and I like historical fiction. This genre is a great way to encourage historical research as well as a way to look at how a character's reputation is enhanced over time. Perhaps there are family stories that your students have heard where one of their relatives has achieved a kind of legendary status or older kids in the neighborhood have become legends because of their athletic prowess. We had a kid in my neighborhood named Jeff Fink who, according to legend, had thrown a ball into orbit! I believed it too. In my film work with Narragansett (Native American) stonemasons, many of them have stories about, as they say, the "legends" in the past . . . those Narragansett masons who performed superhuman feats of strength.

Fables

What lessons of life would students like to share with those who are younger? What animals do they know of or have had as pets would be good "stand-ins" for people? What behaviors have they noticed in these animals lend themselves to teaching lessons to each other? How could their "personalities" be enlisted as examples of behavior they would like to talk about in their *fables*?

Fairy Tales

Magical thinking is part of childhood (and again, adulthood too). What child has not imagined flying, meeting people with magic, and exploring worlds filled with the power to reward the "good" and punish the "bad"? What child has not at some point in their lives, believed in Santa Claus or the tooth fairy?

Mystery

Children are always intrigued by puzzles. After all, who *did* steal those cookies from the cookie jar? Children are natural detectives with a desire to correct injustice and to make a wrong, right. They often feel unfairly accused of something, either by parents or by teachers.

Hero Stories

Did your students ever save a cat or a younger sibling? Did they save a soccer game with a goal in the final minutes? Did they continue a hike at camp, even as their feet were blistering? Did they or anyone they've seen help someone in need of being saved from a bully?

Tragedy and Loss

Did your students ever lose out on a girl or boy they had a crush on? Did your students ever have to leave behind a family home or have they experienced the divorce of parents or the death of an animal? Have your students been bullied, teased, or picked on?

Folklore

The great characters in folklore, like we have already discussed, have very human qualities. In fact, folklore characters probably come from exaggerating stories that people originally told about the people around them. Do your students have funny characters around them, in their family, school, or neighborhood that with a little exaggerating could be folklore characters? I'm sure they do . . . the neighbor who piles his wood perfectly . . . the aunt who has traveled the world . . . the man who emigrated from Russia with the ultimate "green" thumb, who plants and harvests the most beautiful tomatoes.

Myths

Students at a young age are thinking about the great mysteries of life . . . birth, death, weather, earthquakes, and injustices. Mythology has tried to give metaphoric explanation to the "great questions" and to make comprehensible the great forces of nature. Start any study of mythology by giving students a chance to discuss their "big" questions and to playfully speculate about the answers.

> Start any investigation of genre by utilizing what students already know and are thinking about. It's much easier that way . . . students will feel empowered because they will realize *they* have something to share!

Speaking of Genre . . . A Teacher's Horror Story

The sentence continued like a snake, whose tail and head you were not able to see . . . just crawling, slithering, moving in a way you couldn't believe and yet, you were forced to keep looking, because you felt if your eyes glazed over like they wanted to, you would suddenly be struck by the venomous poison of . . . a "run-on" sentence!

7

Grammatical Conventions

Teaching the Grammar Basics of Paragraphs, Sentences, Commas, and Periods

How do you know when to use a period or a comma? How about when to start a new paragraph? It's hard for *us* isn't it? Imagine what it is like for kids!

Rules of punctuation are easy to find. You can look up *comma, run-on sentence,* and *dangling participle* and get a good technical description. But while looking at and memorizing a rule is certainly one way to figure out the often-confusing task of punctuation, I'd like to look at how we can develop an inner understanding of the meaning and placement of paragraphs, sentences, commas, and periods.

Let's play a game! "Red Light, Green Light."

Remember that game? Game leaders call out "red light" or "green light" with their backs turned to those who are trying to replace them. When the light is green, participants rush as quickly as they can but when the leaders suddenly and often sneakily yell "red," they must stop dead in their tracks. If they don't, the offenders have to go back to the beginning.

Imagine the game as a story and each attempted run at the leader, a paragraph. If a racer is able to get to the front without ever being sent back, it's a short story, in fact, a one-paragraph story. The more the challenger is forced to start his or her run anew, the more paragraphs the story has. Each "red," each "stop" is a period on a sentence. If a participant runs through the "sign" and continues after "red" has been called, they are creating a *run-on* sentence and are punished for it. But they have the chance to begin again and to create a new paragraph, in search of a story hopefully ending in victory.

Here's an example with a description of how such a game might look . . .

Once upon a time Kenny who never seemed to win at anything at school was determined to win at the game, "Red Light, Green Light." The leader, Sophie, called out "green" and Kenny rushed forward in a burst of speed. Sensing that Sophie was about to call "red," Kenny readied himself to stop, which he did, on a dime. He guessed correctly the second and third time and now Kenny was close to his goal of overtaking Sophie as the leader. However, as his confidence grew so did his daring and although he once again sensed that Sophie was close to calling out "red," he decided to rush forward and take his chances at replacing her. Sophie, sensing Kenny's impatience, called out "red," with Kenny in stride. He was unable to stop and was sent back to begin his ascent to leadership anew.

As Kenny determinedly began the second phase of his challenge to Sophie and to the others in the game, he thought about the strategy he would take. He could either become more cautious and conservative or he could take his chances with the same aggressive strategy that brought him so close to victory the last time. Kenny chose the latter and began his efforts with a burst of speed that put him within shooting a few short strides of Sophie. . . .

Anyway, you get the picture. Finish the above story any way that makes you happiest. The game is a story: each start from the beginning, a paragraph; and each dash to the finish, within the paragraph, a sentence.

By playing this game and by bringing attention to the parallels between the game and certain grammatical conventions, we can help students internalize the rules of grammar and punctuation. There *are* ways to viscerally and instinctively *feel* when to put a period or a comma and when to start a new sentence, much in the same way we can viscerally understand narrative structure.

> While there are many ways to understand and internalize the rules of periods, sentences, and paragraphs, including reading and hearing literature and directly learning the rules themselves, a more permanent understanding can come from physical and artistic activities that show how grammar and punctuation function.

LOOKING CLOSER AT PARAGRAPHS, SENTENCES, AND COMMAS

Let's eat something. Who doesn't like to eat?

Consider a meal as a story. The courses are its paragraphs. The particular foods in each course are the sentences, and the bites of the food in the courses that are punctuated by small pauses are commas.

One day, prepare a three-course "grammar meal" with your students and their parents for all of you to eat together. Have various appetizers, a few main courses, and some desserts. Point out to your students that they are beginning a story as they sit down to eat. Each course should be considered a paragraph. As they eat the first course, tell students that they are, at that time, part of the first paragraph. Each food they eat in the course can be considered a sentence, and each time they eat one of the foods in the course and something happens, they can punctuate with a comma.

After the meal, have students write about their experience. Again, they are writing a story of the meal with each course they eat a new paragraph and each food, a new sentence. If something happens while they are writing about eating a certain food: say, they drop a fork or are surprised by the taste, have them punctuate it with a comma or use an "and" or "or." For example, "I was eating the sushi with my chopsticks and it dropped to the floor." Have students list the various foods in the individual courses and punctuate the list with commas.

Write a model story on the board.

For Instance . . .

My class and I sat down to a lunch that was made by parents and students.

The first course: the appetizer. In this course we ate garlic bread, a lettuce and tomato salad, and a cup of mushroom soup. First, I picked up my fork and with it, I put a tomato into my mouth. It tasted good and sweet. Next, I put some garlic bread into my mouth. Garlic tastes weird. Then with my big spoon, I had some mushroom soup. As I was eating the mushroom soup, my napkin fell off my lap, and I became so flustered that my spoon tipped over and soup spilled all over my lap. When I tried to pick up the napkin, I noticed that my entire class was laughing at me.

The next course was the main course. We had hot dogs, hamburgers, meat loaf, and vegetarian burritos. The hot dogs tasted great. The hamburgers were a little dry. I didn't touch the vegetarian burritos, because I only like chicken burritos. (Notice the comma separating a statement from its explanation.)

Our desserts were great. We had ice cream, chocolate chip cookies, Jell-O, and a great fruit salad. The fruit salad had peaches, grapes, bananas, and strawberries in it. I first ate the cookies, then the Jell-O, and then the ice cream. The ice cream melted and poured off the spoon onto my hand and arm. By the time the dinner finished, I was a mess.

USING ACTIVITIES AS STORY IDEAS

Take students on a walk around the school. Start first in your classroom, walk down the hall, into the gym, and then into the lunchroom. It really doesn't matter what places you visit as long as you choose distinct places for an activity to take place or to see something. Write about what you do during each part of your walk. Each room visited can be considered a new paragraph. The complete walk is the story of your "tour," and descriptions of what happens in each classroom are punctuated when describing one particular thing you are doing, for example, looking at an atlas in the library or doing three or more things in one of the rooms. Curious about where Zanzibar was, I took the atlas out, opened it, looked at a map of Africa, and finally satisfied my curiosity.

Do the same as above with a walk around the neighborhood. Here, the walk is the story; the different "stopping points" such as parks, monuments, and interesting buildings are your paragraphs; and as you describe what you do and see at each particular place, these are your sentences. When you string together three or more things that happen at these sites, use commas as you describe them.

For Instance . . .

Our class walked around the neighborhood today. First we stopped at Bailey Park. At Bailey Park there are swings, climbing bars, sand boxes, and slides. We went on the slide first. Then we went climbing. I was able to make it from one side to the other without falling. My friend James made it too, but Tyrone didn't and he fell.

Our next stop was the vegetable and fruit store. We bought peaches, bananas, grapes, and mangos for a fruit salad that we wanted to make later. Our teacher asked us to tell him how much everything would cost. We weighed the fruit on the scales and with a pencil we brought, we figured it out.

Taking trips and dividing the trips into parts is a good way to work on the distinctions between story, paragraphs, and sentences. Having students create a file system is another good way to make the distinctions between story, sentences, and paragraphs clear. For example, create a file system for a large topic say, sports. This is your *story*. The individual sports are your paragraphs (baseball, basketball, etc.) and your pictures and articles within each of those files of say, people batting or fielding various positions are your sentences.

When we start a story we are beginning a journey. Journeys have phases or paragraphs. These paragraphs or phases in the journey consist of smaller elements, sentences, and often these smaller elements have still smaller elements that have so much in common with each other that they are listed, with the help of commas.

REGARDING RUN-ON SENTENCES

One problem that we've all noticed with students is the *run-on* sentence. You know, the sentence that strings along about 10 things the writer has done, like: I went to school and I got caught in the rain and I got wet and before I got to school I was sneezing and I had a cold and I called my mom at school and she came and got me and she brought me home but first we went to the doctor who . . . OK, you get it, I'm sure. Obviously, many of the components of the above sentence could have been their own sentences.

In a *run on* sentence, two or more independent clauses are fused together (hence the term *fused sentences*). OK, now we know technically what the problem is, but I ask you: What is really wrong with it? I ask you that because while we have a "sense" that it is wrong to endlessly string along activities, events, etc., with the help of multiple "ands," it would be easier for children to understand and for us to teach if we really understood how a *run-on* sentence either impedes or enhances the reader's understanding and enjoyment of a text. After all, that is why we are writing isn't it, unless we are writing a journal or a diary for our eyes only, of course.

Using a *run-on* sentence is "overloading the circuits." When the brain is overloaded, it no longer has the ability to understand and to integrate new knowledge. Our brain shuts down not unlike a computer crashing when we ask it to do too many functions at once or when a fuse blows when we attach too many electrical appliances into a circuit. Our brain filters a large percentage of the information that routinely bombards it. There is a reason why at a wine tasting you are offered a piece of bread or a cracker in between wines. It's to clean the palette before the next offering.

A *run-on* sentence, simply said, is hard to digest and therefore difficult to appreciate. No matter how good something is, you lose the ability to embrace it, appreciate it, and to make it a part of you if you are given too much, too quickly.

So, how do we create activities that will physically, viscerally, and metaphorically demonstrate the differences between a sentence that is easily read and appreciated rather than one that feels like you are watching a mile-long freight train slowly rolling off into the high, southwestern desert . . . while you're waiting to cross the tracks!

Here are some ideas:

- Have students write and read the longest *run-on* sentence they can create and then have the other students talk about how their minds and bodies felt while they listened. Ask students to tell you what details they remember from the sentence.
- If you have the facilities, fill a sink or a bucket with water. Find a piece of wood that can float in the water and, while reading some of the students' *run-on* sentences, put cans of vegetables on the wood for each clause in the sentence. At some point the wood will sink or the objects will tumble into the water.
- Take a paper bag and fill it with a book for each clause that is part of a *run-on* sentence. With each new book, try lifting the bag until, inevitably, the contents of the bag are too heavy and the bag breaks.
- In pairs, have students throw balls back and forth to each other until they are so tired they have to stop. What began as an enjoyable activity becomes boring and tiring, much like a *run-on* sentence.
- Ask students to think and write about a time when they ate something that tasted so good they couldn't stop eating it. What were the consequences?
- Have students orally give a book report or describe a sports event they participated in without stopping for a period. Ask the others what it felt to hear.

Commas

Commas are about stacking things together and combining. Think about stacking and combining when you are trying to create activities that will support this understanding. Here are some activities that will help to teach these ideas:

- Divide up the class into pairs. Create as much room between the pairs as possible. (You might want to do this activity in the gym or lunchroom.) Have students bring in cans of food (corn, beans, etc.) to see which team can handle the largest number in their arms. When this activity is over, have each group write a sentence listing all of the different types of cans they held. (This is where the commas come in.)

  Example: Our team carried cans of corn, peas, string beans, garbanzo beans, black-eyed peas, and navy beans.

- Line up your class and write a list of the different colors of shirts worn that day . . . or those with brown eyes, black hair, etc.

  Example: In my class, there were many kinds of shirts worn today. Steve wore blue, Ravena wore green, Sopia wore purple, and so on.

- Have students write a sentence listing the sports they like or the TV programs they enjoy.

  Example: I like to play basketball, baseball, soccer, and football.

- Have students create a fantasy pizza, ice cream sundae, or sandwich, listing all the ingredients they would include.

  Example: I would like to have a pizza with mushrooms, sun-dried tomatoes, feta cheese, red peppers, and artichoke hearts.

- List all the students in the class who are wearing the color blue.

OK, you get the point . . . lists need commas.
Another thing about commas: They separate independent clauses like . . .

- o "I went to the ball game, but it started to rain and I had to go home" or . . .
- o "Yesterday was my parents' anniversary, so my brother and I took them out for dinner."

Both of these are examples of what could have been two independent sentences, brought together to explain one of them.

- Have students think of things they should have or could have done and create a reason why they didn't do it.

  For example: "I should have done my homework, but my grandparents came over," or "I could have gone to the rock concert, but I got really sick with the flu."

- Have students talk about something they did and why they did it.

  For example: "Yesterday was the last day of school, so my friends and I went to the beach to celebrate," or "I realized that I had to pack for summer camp, so I told my friends that I couldn't go to the movie."

Sometimes commas are used to explain things, like when the words *while*, *because*, *if*, and *when* start a sentence. For example: "While I often like to go swimming on Saturdays, it was just too cold yesterday for a jump into the pool," or "Because the snow was dry, it was hard to make snowballs."

Again, commas are used to help set up an explanation, an excuse, a reason.

- Have students explain why they didn't do something they were supposed to do. (*Because*)

  Example: "I didn't go to school today, because I had a very bad cold."
- Have students explain why they didn't do something they ordinarily would do. (*While*)

  Example: "While Mondays are usually the day I go to step dancing, Wanda told me that the teacher was sick so I didn't bother going."
- Have students write about planning to do something, after or when something else has happened. (*When*)

  Example: "We were all ready to go on the picnic, when the thunder roared and the rain fell."
- Have students speculate about doing something based on something else. (*If*)

  Example: "I could get straight A's if only my brother didn't listen to the radio when I studied.

There are many other explanations for why or why not to use commas. There are plenty of Web sites and books devoted to punctuation. I just wanted to introduce you to some ideas about how you might make the "rules" more meaningful, understandable, and more fun to comprehend for students. It is always helpful to realize too that many modern writers ignored a lot of the conventions we've been talking about. But they knew what those conventions were and decided to break with them consciously and purposefully.

Speaking of writers who broke with convention, many were able to experiment because they created in the context of a supportive community . . . the Bloomsbury Circle at the turn of 20th century Great Britain, the salons of Paris in the 1920s, the coffeehouses of the "beat" writers in 1950s New York and San Francisco, and perhaps . . . Ms. Allen's fifth grade class in 2010.

8

Encouraging a Culture of Writing in Your Classroom

Creating a Writer's Studio and Salon

College and professional athletes eat together, watch films of previous games together, and lift weights together. Lawyers discuss cases, fill their offices with law books, and attend seminars and lectures on new court decisions. Artists often look at each other's work, listen to music while they paint or sculpt, surround themselves with interesting objects, and read biographies of older artists. Those in the construction trades look at builder's magazines, talk to each other at building supply stores, and look at each other's work. How about student writers? What kind of a writing culture are they immersed in?

People who share common professions have similar interests and needs. Writers usually need both communal and individual space to thrive. They need space both for solitary exploration and for the opportunity to share with others.

In this chapter, we will look at the various ways we can support student writing by creating—along with input from students—a classroom culture that is conducive to thinking, discussing, experimenting, planning, and cooperating. Your room should physically accommodate and reflect these various needs.

Most of our classrooms serve as "multipurpose" rooms where many dieties are worshipped. There is the G—d of math, the G—d of social studies, the G—d of science, and so on. In elementary school, as you well know, there are many skills being taught under one roof and in one classroom.

So how can we create a space for writing in a room where so much else is going on? We will look at both the physical makeup of the classroom and at the way in which your day is organized.

What kind of environment do you feel good in? What makes you feel relaxed . . . creative? What kind of environment supports taking risks? Where do you feel most comfortable working on "craft"? And of course we should ask students the same questions and let their answers help dictate the way the room is set up.

CREATING A WRITER'S STUDIO TO SERVE INDIVIDUAL NEEDS

Have you ever looked at a writer's studio? They are all different, but they also have some things in common. Usually, they are filled with books and papers, and they often contain personal items, such as presents given to them and small artifacts of daily life: jars filled with change, pens and pencils; maybe a glass for beverages; an old plate with crumbs. Sometimes there is a CD or tape player, a computer for some, and paper for others. Some have a couch or chair. Most authors are very particular about their lighting. After all, the studio is like a small, personal home.

Let's look at the various elements that compose one's individual writing space.

Lighting

Lighting is very important for many of us. The glare of fluorescent lights creates a "buzz," or "hum" that even as a child I read as "Rush!" Writing, as we have talked about, is not a "sprint," unless you have a newspaper or grant deadline . . . or unless you are a child being tested! It is an activity that requires thought, reflection, and time. Overhead lighting never helps me relax. It always makes me feel like I am being "watched" and moved along quickly. I never and still don't feel comfortable under fluorescent lights. They make me feel like I'm in the motor vehicle bureau or in any of a number of government offices. Softer, less direct lighting would be better for a student's *writer's studio*. Lamps around the classroom help to establish a more "homey" feeling, one that is more human and personal and not as much associated with commercial or business space and activities.

Check out your favorite coffeehouses. Most have lamps, not fluorescent or overhead lighting. It's funny how most of us prefer non-direct lighting at home, but in school we tolerate the lighting of an office cubicle. If it isn't a safety issue, let your students bring in a small desk lamp. The great Chilean poet Pablo Neruda wrote an "ode" to his lamp, telling the world how important his lamp was to his work. Permitting a child to bring in a small lamp allows them to have some personal control over their environment and helps to make them feel more relaxed and "at home."

One way to distinguish your writing time from the other designated times in your day is to turn off the overhead lights and let the softer lighting prevail. This will send a clear message that "writer's studio behavior" is expected.

The Desk

When you are in "writer's studio time," all textbooks should be removed from desks. It is so easy to be distracted from writing. Even as I write this, I am fighting the urge to check e-mails, to clean my desk, to look through and worry about my bills. The less we have on our desk to distract us, the better.

That is not to say there shouldn't be anything on our desks at all. Give students permission to put some familiar items in front of them. Depending on the student, they might choose anything from a small stuffed animal to a signed baseball. Small intimate objects, again, create a homey feeling, one that is comfortable and familiar and one that can provide small bits of distraction when needed.

Students also should have one or two pens or pencils they particularly like when they start their work. There is nothing more distracting to them or others as when they rifle through their desks in a chaotic and often frustrating attempt to find their writing utensils. Getting out a specific pencil or pen should be like cleaning off the desk, changing the lighting, and placing one's "special" object; all part of the ritual of beginning the writer's work. If you ask students to set aside their writing pen or pencil in a corner of their desk or in a special box, they will always be able to locate it (hopefully), and it will also begin to acquire a special significance.

The same is true with the writer's notebook. Having a special, easily available book for writing is a good idea. Some schools, however, make a big deal about giving it out, coloring it, and decorating it. I wouldn't. If your students want to do that, fine. Most grown-up writers that I know don't. It is my opinion that the more we make the process of writing seem like second nature and not "special," the better we are. The more we "celebrate" our new notebooks, the more pressure we put on our students. It often feels contrived to me when we decorate our writer's notebook much like a kindergarten graduation.

A quick word about the pencil sharpener migration . . . you know what I'm talking about . . . the ever-continuing march to the sharpener? I recommend that students work in pen, but if that's not possible, have two or three sharpeners around the room and when your students come in to school and socialize in the morning, it is also time to sharpen. If pencil sharpening stays a problem, I would ask your class to decide how to best solve this distraction.

Don't Forget to Take a Break

> Sometimes you have to just drop what you are thinking about to get the answers you are looking for.

A "break" *is* an important part of the writing process. There are many moments while writing when a break is important to "clear one's head." Most religions use some form of moving or walking as part of their mental exercise . . . yoga, tai chi, the labyrinth in some churches, the Zen "walk." We all know that when stressed, it's good to just get out of the house for a while. Sometimes seemingly insurmountable problems find solution when we give them a new perspective by simply changing location. For me, a walk around my house, cleaning dishes, or going to the beach will help me to break through some obstacle I'm encountering in my writing. And yet, knowing this, how often do we give our students the opportunity to do the same?

Some of you reading this might say, "Oh, I can't trust my students to walk around the classroom. They will talk with each other. They will disrupt their neighbors. They will play with inappropriate things."

Let's ask students what *they* need. Do they need breaks? If so, what would they like to be able to do? What are the things they worry about if breaks are permitted? How can we (they) come up with the ground rules for taking some time to "clear heads"? You might be surprised at the clarity of their responses. I'm sure some of their responses would be similar to yours. "Don't talk with anyone." "Don't make excessive noise." "Get back to work after a certain amount of time away." Having students come up with mutually agreed upon rules for their "break time" will go a long way toward having them "invest" in creating the kind culture of writing that you are interested in creating.

Some students might suggest having chairs and couches around the room. I personally think it's a good idea. A comfortable chair or couch for sitting quietly for a few minutes can really reinvigorate the spirit and refresh the mind. Should students be able to continue writing while on the chair or couch? I would like to say yes. However I worry, as I'm sure you do, about fights over "prime" real estate and the temptation to talk and to be distracted while on the floor or sitting on a couch with a buddy. Again, you can put it to your students. "How can we make sure these things don't happen?" How about a schedule for sitting on chairs and couches: If you talk, you go back to your seat or move to the end of the line on the "special places" schedule? Obviously, if one or more students are continually mischievous or are forever wandering around the classroom, then you have some issues that may require individual conferencing to determine the problem. (There is a lot of literature on conferencing so I've decided not to go into it here.) As you know, disruptive or distracting behavior often comes from frustration and sometimes a slight "push" is all that is needed to get your students back on track.

When I take a break from writing, I like to have things to look at other than my own writing. I just got up as I was writing this paragraph and went into the kitchen where Sunday's *New York Times* was piled up. The front cover of the business section had an article about Sean Comb's business ventures. I looked at it briefly, and then I returned to my desk.

Sometimes I look at my book of baseball statistics. Whatever it is, many writers like to be momentarily (and sometimes more than that) distracted by pictures and/or text. So, perhaps, it might be OK to have a few magazines or books to glance at while students are walking around the classroom. Or maybe we might want to think about what to put on our walls . . . maps . . . news articles . . . photos? The kind of pictures and charts we talked about earlier in this book? Students should realize, though, that these distractions are not a substitute for writing but rather a temporary break so that writing can flow again.

Creating a writer's studio in a shared space is not easy. Luckily you have 25 or so others to help you figure it out!

CREATING A SALON TO SHARE WORK AND IDEAS

A large part of learning how to become a writer is having the opportunity to discuss your writing, to listen to and critique other writing, and to be able to share one's intellectual and personal concerns in a safe and supportive atmosphere. Essentially, we are talking about creating a *salon*. Salons were (and are) gatherings, usually in people's houses, where writers, artists, and intellectuals gather to share their work and ideas. Mabel Dodge Luhan in the early part of the 20th century ran a famous Greenwich Village salon where writers and artists, famous even to this day, felt the support and companionship they needed to thrive. In Paris in the 1920s, Gertrude Stein did the same. Talk to your students about the history of salons and how to create them.

What are the components of a salon and how can we help create the same effect in our classrooms?

Salons are supportive and at times challenging artistic environments where everyone feels their work benefits from the support and advice they receive from others. Salon participants have often felt they were part of something important; that they were "creating a new world," a new "culture" with their art and/or writings. They enjoyed what they were doing. They had fun. They valued visual art, music, dance, and writing and considered them to be important for the health of society.

Morning circle is a good place to really get things going. It is a good place to create a safe environment for talking about what is happening in everyone's world. Listen to any new music lately? Learn any new skateboard tricks? Discover any new video games? How are things at home? Any dreams? Anyone have drawings they'd like to show us? Is anyone reading anything new? What do you think of it? How's the writing going for everyone? Anyone watch anything on TV that you liked? Why did you like it? This early circle can take up to 15 minutes. It's really a "check-in." Everyone should be heard even if it means formalizing it by passing around a stick or a stuffed animal.

This kind of discussion sets the mood for the day and allows students to get talking and thinking and reflecting on how they spend their time after and before school. It also shows them that you and the other students are interested in hearing about each other's interests. When I'm working with a new class at school, I always start by having students introduce themselves to me (one at a time) and then having them tell me one thing they like to do. This isn't much of an introduction and can take some time, but it is the first step in letting them know that someone cares about them.

Start with a "writer's circle" before entering into your time for writing. This circle is specifically for writing issues and ideas; it lets students know they are entering into a specific time of their day. Start with reading a portion of a text pertinent to the issue you are working on at the time: beginnings, sequences, genre, etc. Discuss the piece of writing and see how and why students liked or disliked it. Ask students to consider how it could have been done better or differently. Students need this time to reflect on the writing of others as they fine-tune their own skills. This is also the time to read quotes by writers on writing, to discuss writers' biographies, and to notice how many different kinds of writing there are. Another idea during this time is to encourage students to write letters to authors who they like. They can ask the authors questions about writing, ideas for dealing with difficulties encountered while writing, and so on.

Use your salon time to question students about their writing. Ask if they are having difficulty with some aspect of their writing and, if so, see if you can get the other students to help. Have some students read their latest "work" and begin a *critique* process. It is always helpful to have an agreed upon method of and language for critique that can be followed throughout the year. You can formulate this at the beginning of the year with the help of the students. Perhaps it could be that any critique needs to start with a compliment or two.

A QUICK WORD ON COLLECTIVE SPACE . . .

There should be space to gather as a group. A rug is the best unless your students are too old to sit on the floor. I like a Persian or Turkish rug the best. The colors and patterns are interesting, and there is always something to look at in case a student gets bored or wants to "space out" for a bit. Rugs that are "fluffy" or those with a lot of things to pull . . . need I finish the sentence?

Once students have had "sharing" time, it is time for individual work; time to go into *writer's studio* mode. Before doing that, however, you should discuss what is expected for this particular period on this particular day. Are students working on beginnings, on persuasive letters, on paragraphs? Do they have any questions?

During studio time, some soft music helps to calm things down and makes the transition from salon to studio time easier. Look around the room and see who is having trouble getting started. A short conversation started by, "Having any trouble?" "What are you working on?" "Need any help?" usually gets things moving.

After a number of minutes (your call), have students "conference" with their writing partner. All students should have a writing partner, but one that changes every month or so. At first, try to put together students who have relatively equal skills. As the year progresses, let the more advanced students help those less skilled as writers. Try having students choose their partner for one month and as the year draws to a close, put more equal writers together again.

Many professional writers have *writing buddies*, people to whom they show their writing and discuss issues; someone whom they depend upon for critique. Tell your students that. Take 15 minutes of so for conferencing. Allow the partners to choose their spots in the room to talk and listen to each other. To make sure the conversation is appropriate, wander around the room, listen to, and participate in the conversation.

After the conferencing and before students go again into "studio mode," have a short check-in. With students back in their seats, ask if anyone is having difficulty or has discovered something either individually or with their partner. Give some more time for studio time (your call), and then end the writing session.

Have a final salon session on the rug. If you feel like it and can easily do it, give out some water or juice to make students feel more "adult," and begin a discussion about the work just accomplished. What did they find easy or difficult? Where do they feel they need more help? If something comes up that you feel you can deal with at that moment—for instance, a question about description—handle it then with a discussion or an exercise. If not, make a mental note to deal with it in tomorrow's session. Ask some students to volunteer to read some of their work and initiate a critique session.

After the allotted writing time is used, discuss what if anything you want students to work on at home. Although I don't want to get into the homework versus no homework debate here, I do feel that it is valuable for students after school to make entries into their writer's notebook . . . maybe about something they are reading, something they've noticed, something they've dreamt, or something they've learned in a studio or salon session. This will keep the process of reflection going and will give your students something to share in morning salon.

Please don't be turned off by the seeming rigidity of the above sessions. I also feel that discussions of and the use of writing should occur spontaneously throughout the day. This can happen whenever writing is called for or whenever you can reinforce a writing lesson with something from another "discipline." My intention here, given your time constraints, is to provide a fairly organized approach about how to devote a part of your day to the writer's work.

9

Endings

Putting a Period on a Story Means More Than a Period!

As *we* (dear readers) prepare to say "good-bye," we understand once more (I hope) that endings are always difficult, aren't they? Think of all the songs that tell us so: "What's So Good About Goodbye?"; "Hello, Goodbye"; "Breaking Up is Hard to Do"; "Crazy"; and "In the Wee Small Hours of the Morning" (my favorite). Did you know that there is an entire Web site devoted to "break-up" songs?

Endings can be painful, confusing, contrived, and liberating. Endings of student stories can be all of the above as well. It is really difficult to end a story. After all, while some say death is an ending, others say it is a beginning. Ends don't really naturally happen. Life just changes rather than ends. Flowers die and go to seed. Relationships, rather than just stopping, usually morph into something new (even if they live only as memories). But then again, things do sometimes come to, at least what appears to be, an end. Groups of people disperse. People awaken. Storms are over. Sports events finish. Homework gets done and dishes get washed.

In student writing, events are usually tied up rather simply, if at all. Often the endings of students' stories go something like . . . "And then we all went home" or "And that was the end of the party" or "And now you understand how a caterpillar morphs into a butterfly." Most of the time student endings are abrupt departures from the story line. Their writings get to a cliff and leap. Happily finished with an assignment, they usually exit their stories as quickly as they leave the classroom on a Friday afternoon . . . or as quickly as a teacher does.

What is the purpose of an ending anyway?

> The purpose of an ending is to allow us to "move on" to something new, such as a book, article, activity, or chore. It needs to make us feel satisfied; feeling like the work we've put into a text has been "worth it" and that there has been a good "payoff," a momentary sense of finality.

We want to feel like we haven't been cheated or led on, disappointed with how the elements of the story have been resolved. We want to know that the author has accounted for the characters we've come to care about. We want to leave a text feeling like the author took the time to make the ending consistent with the tone and feeling of the rest of the piece (or that the author consciously made an attempt not to do so). We want to feel that the author found a way to make the difficult transition to the *ending* somehow OK and believable or at least interesting. The ending often also makes the author's point of view clear about the issues that gets put into play.

How do we get students to understand how endings work? First, let's come up with some activities that demonstrate what an ending is and how it functions. Remember, the more students realize they have experienced and "felt" an ending, the easier it will be for them to replicate that understanding with their own work.

Here are some activities that will help students in this regard:

- Have students clean the classroom at the end of the day. (They should do that at the end of everyday anyway, but that's another book.) They should delineate needs and responsibilities. After the room is cleaned, have students discuss how they did. If they think they did a good job, ask them why. If they think the job was not finished, ask them the same question. If they think the job was done successfully, usually they will talk about how everything is neatly put away. If they think it wasn't done well, it usually means that some things need better care. Remind them that similar criteria are usable for judging whether or not a story ended successfully, that is by looking at which characters or situations have been metaphorically left out in the middle of the floor and not "put away."
- Talk with students about the endings in movies, books, or TV programs they've seen. Which ones did they like? Which ones didn't they like? Why? How did the endings leave them feeling? Why? What happened to the characters?
- Have students talk or write about a game they saw or participated in and have them pay special attention to the ending. The game can be a

sporting event or a board game or even a video game. Was it dramatic or anticlimactic Was it surprising or was the ending predictable?

- Ask students if they have ever watched a storm come in and then leave? What did it feel like? How did the storm end?
- How does the school year end? How about summer camp?
- How about an amusement park ride . . . how does *it* end? Is there a build up to the end? Is the scariest part right before the end?
- Do your students remember any funerals? What were they like? (Obviously, be careful with this issue and don't push it if it brings up too many traumatic memories.)
- Do students remember losing or throwing away a particular stuffed animal or toy? Have them write or tell about their involvement with a particular toy and how it got lost and then how they felt about its loss.
- Have students make an art or craft project and discuss the different stages of its creation from beginning to end. It could be a pot from clay, a painting, something from wood, etc.
- Have students ever left a good friend? Have students been left by a friend or a family member? Have students ever decided that someone wasn't a friend anymore? Did someone who considered another person a friend, decide that person was no longer "cool" enough to be a friend?

What do the above endings have in common? How are they different from one another?

Now it's time to write some endings. First, let's try telling folktales, fairy tales, or memoirs verbally. Have students end them in new ways. If they've ended tragically, make them humorous. If they were predictable, make the ending unexpected. How do you make an ending comedic, tragic, or dramatic anyway? Let's take a story we all know and see how.

We'll start by using *The Boy Who Cried Wolf* to see how different endings can change the nature and meaning of a story. You know the story I'm sure . . . the lonely shepherd boy shouts loudly that a wolf is near him so that the town's people will come around. Each time they heed the shepherd's call, there's no wolf. When a wolf finally does come around the shepherd, no one comes to the boy's aid and the wolf tragically devours the flock.

So let's look at a few ways we might change the story's ending.

SAMPLE DRAMATIC ENDING

The shepherd calls and calls as the wolf eyes him for its noon-time meal. Those who have continually heard the shepherd's calls and have rushed to his aid, now ignore his pleas. The wolf circles the shepherd who is trying desperately to block the path of the wolf on its way to the sheep. The shepherd, realizing that he has used up his trust with the villagers, calls out once more, his voice now full of fear. An itinerant hunter, who is passing through town for the first time, hears the boy, runs out into the pasture with his gun, and kills the wolf just as it was ready to pounce on a baby lamb!

SAMPLE COMEDIC ENDING

The shepherd calls and calls and calls and yet the villagers who have heard the pleas before, ignore the young boy. The wolf, ready to pounce on one of the fat sheep, turns briefly and sees that the boy is desperately and unsuccessfully yelling for help. Thinking for a moment, the wolf tells the boy that it's his style that is all wrong. When he yells for help the wolf, a real "know-it-all," tells the boy that he should be nonchalant and to act as if he doesn't care. "No one helps someone unless they think that someone doesn't really need it," says the wolf. The boy, recognizing an opportunity, flatters the wolf into showing him how to call out for help in the "proper" way. "Try it like this," the wolf says. The wolf imitates the boy's voice perfectly, calling out in a very relaxed manner, "Wolf here, Wolf here. Come help if you'd like. I'm really quite fine without your help though." Upon hearing that, the townspeople actually run up into the field where the boy and his flock are nearly goners. As they reach the pasture with rifles in hand, the wolf realizes what it has done and runs as fast as it can, away from what would have been a fine, fine lunch.

SAMPLE SURPRISE ENDING

The shepherd calls . . . and no one comes. The wolf is ready to pounce on a sheep and have its meal when it decides to first sit down next to the boy. The wolf asks the shepherd why he continually gives wolves a bad name by continually saying that the wolf was about to eat him and his sheep. "It really hurts me and my brothers and sisters that no one likes us." "Sure," the wolf continues, "every once in a while we gets hungry. Who doesn't? All we do then is take out a few sickly sheep that wouldn't be long for the world anyway and have them for dinner. Most of the time we wolves, like any other creature, are just hanging out trying to enjoy ourselves." The boy's jaw dropped as he realizes that to his surprise, the wolf can talk and also how much he and the villagers had misread wolves all these years. He vows that from then on, he will protect the reputation of the wolf and will tell anyone he can that wolves really aren't as bad as everyone thought. The wolf says that it is deeply grateful, but unfortunately it *is* really hungry and with one quick bite . . . it eats the boy.

SAMPLE ROMANTIC ENDING

The boy calls again and again. No one comes. A young woman the shepherd's age happened to be nearby, picking flowers and gathering water from a well, when she passes by the wolf and the boy. The boy and the girl's eyes meet . . . love at first sight. The songs of the birds become louder and the once cloudy sky clears. The boy and the girl are in love and the feeling of their love permeates the entire valley. Even the wolf recognizes the romantic attraction that illuminates the world. The wolf smiles, its big white teeth glistening, as it lies down dreamily next to the sheep, leaving the sheep and the new lovers alone to bask in the bliss of their mutual attraction.

What makes a story humorous, tragic, romantic, or surprising? This is a huge question and one that is and has been discussed for centuries; but one thing is clear, it is usually the ending that determines how the story is viewed and "summed up."

Let's see if your students can take a stab changing an ending to our story by making it comedic. Kids certainly understand humor. To prepare for this task, ask them to tell you what they've seen or read that they consider funny. Ask why they think something is funny. Was it that the characters kept slipping and falling in spite of acting like they were "all that"? Often humor comes at the expense of someone who is "showing off" or "evil" like the wolf in the previous, comedic version of the Aesop fable. When a lot of things go wrong at the same time, it also makes for humor because as they say . . . the best laid plans. Who, for instance, hasn't enjoyed the comic disaster scene in movies when the dog runs through the wedding toppling the table, which topples the cake, which lands on the mother-in-law, who screams and her plate, full of food, goes up in the air and lands on the sleeping grandfather? Humor sometimes depends on the "world going wild" in unpredictable, yet usually mostly harmless ways.

So how would a new ending make our or another story comedic?

BEWARE OF TRAGIC ENDINGS

You might want to be careful with this type of ending unless your students are old enough to have a discussion about this topic without it affecting them too badly. Tragedy happens when mortality is introduced into a story or when characters fail at something in spite of their best efforts.

Tragedy also happens when one experiences loss, for example, parent's divorcing, friends leaving, grandparents getting sick.

WHAT ABOUT SURPRISE ENDINGS?

Surprise occurs when some predictable logic is voided and a person, natural phenomena, or inanimate object acts in a completely unpredicted manner . . . like the wolf eating the boy even after the boy recognizes the error of his ways. The old *Twilight Zone* TV show was great for surprises . . . with inanimate objects taking on a life of their own and characters appearing at surprising moments (like on an airplane wing). Have students ever been surprised? Of course they have . . . by visits, by presents . . . who knows what else? Have them tell you the story of the surprise and see if you can help them analyze why they were surprised. Maybe a dog showed up at their doorstep, and they took it in.

WHAT ABOUT HAPPY OR ROMANTIC ENDINGS?

A romantic or happy ending doesn't necessarily end with two people walking off into the sunset. It happens when all the threads of a story seem to tie up as perfectly as the veritable bow on a package. All the characters get what they worked for, except those whose motives were "impure." For instance, when the money comes through to save the family from eviction or when the bad but loveable baseball team wins the championship for the coach who is in the hospital with a terrible disease . . . and the disease is cured by the joy he experienced from victory . . . OK, OK, let's not get carried away here! A happy ending is usually what students know best, although it often doesn't really reflect their real-life experiences. We should be careful with the overuse of this type of ending, although it is OK to use since students have experienced this type of ending in their own readings. Take *Cinderella*, for instance, where virtue is rewarded and evil is punished . . . simple, but not a bad teaching tool.

So again, have students try out different endings for the same and for different stories. Go over what makes endings tragic, surprising, romantic, or happy, prompting their memories with discussion.

SERVING STUDENTS AND THEIR INTENT

Students should be taught to look at what purpose they want their endings to serve. What is the story's intent? How do they want their audience to feel about their story and the characters they've created?

If your student's intent was to validate a proverb, for instance, "A stitch in time saves nine," then their ending should reflect that. Do they want to reward a character's kindness? If yes, their ending should reflect that. The same is true for other motives. The ending ultimately shares with the audience how the author feels about the world they've created, the questions and issues addressed, and the characters introduced. Helping students become conscious of the choices they are making and the ramifications of those choices is an essential part of our work as writing instructors. There is no place where the gravity of this work is clearer than here, with the crafting of endings. Asking students to commit to a point of view in their writing is very, very helpful and at times quite difficult.

A good way to help students develop an awareness of how their endings can serve their intent is to get a list of proverbs and have students pick one on which they agree. Ask students to write a story that supports this proverb's point of view. Share these writings with the class and have the other students tell the author whether or not they feel the story supported the proverb's point of view. To continue with this discussion, have students look at movies, books, and cartoons to assess whether the author's point of view is supported by the choice of endings. Additionally, a solid background in folktales and fairy tales should demonstrate how an ending proves a point by rewarding the good, punishing the evil, and redeeming the fallen.

And now I am coming to my ending. How should my ending reinforce what I feel was the point of this book? Well, why not a story?

Nasrudin, the wise fool of the Middle East, gets richer and richer and his houses on either side of the border seemingly grow bigger each day Every week or so Nasrudin crosses this border with his donkey. Try as he might, the border guard just can't figure out what Nasrudin is smuggling across the border that allows him to accumulate such wealth.

After the border guard retires, he is drinking coffee in a café with Nasrudin. He inhales tobacco from the hookah, exhales and says, "Nasrudin, you are a wealthy man. I never have seen you do any work in your life and each week you are crossing the border with your donkey and while I am sure you must be smuggling something, I have after all these years found nothing. Now that I'm retired, won't you tell me what it was that you were illegally taking over the border?

Nasrudin smiles at his once adversary and now friend and, as he exhales the smoke from his hookah, he says simply, "Donkeys."

And so it is my new friends and readers, the knowledge that our students' need for good writing is often right under their and our noses! Our job is to point it out.

Please try some of the ideas in this book, and let me know how you do. Of course if you come up with anything new based on some of my ideas, please share it with me. Even authors of books on writing need new ideas, you know!

Thanks for giving me your time and attention. I know in this busy, crazy world that both are in short supply.

The End.

Index